ELECTRICAL CHRISTIANITY
A Revolutionary Guide to Jesus' Teachings and Spiritual Enlightenment

By L. Ron Gardner

CONTENTS

Introduction

Electrical Christianity and the Gospel

If Jesus Christ were alive today, I believe he would update the Gospel and teach the "brand" of Christianity that I introduce and elaborate on in this book—Electrical Christianity. Jesus' updated teachings would likely mirror those of Electrical Christianity because spiritual energy is electrical in nature, and if Jesus, a spiritual genius, knew about electricity, he would almost certainly make it a point to explain the principles of spiritual life via the parallel principles of electricity.

The principles of electricity are implicit in the Bible and in the teachings of various mystics, Christian and otherwise; but in my extensive study of the esoteric spiritual traditions, I have never encountered a mystic who does more than allude to the relationship between electricity and spirituality. None whom I've read has explicated this relationship. In this book I will do so.

In addition to elucidating the parallel between electricity and *true* Christianity, I also explain exactly how a *disciple*, a true Christian, can apply this parallel to his spiritual practice. In short, I correlate the principles of a simple electrical circuit (Ohm's Law) with the practice of the Eucharist (Holy Communion), the foremost mystical discipline.

The Practice of True Holy Communion

Mainstream Christian churches are guilty of an egregious sin: They do not teach their members how to commune with the

Deity and receive His Blessing Power, the Holy Spirit. There can be no true religion, no real spirituality, without contact with and reception of God's Spirit-power. This book provides clear-cut, in-depth instructions on how to directly "plug into" the Divine Being, the Holy One, and literally "pull down" His Power. Grace is *not* an abstract principle; it *is* the palpable experience of God's Spirit-power—and anyone who religiously (or devotedly and intensely) practices the discipline of true Holy Communion that I present in this book can experience the descent of Divine Power, the Holy Spirit.

The *true* Eucharist, the practice of Holy Communion (which, in its "awakened" form implies reception of the Holy Spirit), is the very heart of mystical Christianity—and I maintain that it is the foremost method for attaining salvation (spiritual en-Light-enment). Furthermore, if the practice of Holy Communion is augmented with an understanding of Electrical Christianity (Ohm's Law applied to Christianity), it becomes an even more potent en-Light-enment tool. Disciples of the Truth who meditate on the parallels between the Eucharist and Ohm's Law are sure to increase their understanding of spiritual life and improve their spiritual practice.

Ohm's Law and Spiritual Energy

Ohm's Law, the mathematical equation or formula for an electrical circuit, was discovered in 1827, and is the key to understanding the relationship between electrical and spiritual energy. Although I briefly touch upon other aspects of electricity, the central focus of my thesis is the correlation between Ohm's Law and spirituality. I can't prove that Ohm's Law holds true for spiritual energy, but even if it doesn't perfectly correlate with the spiritual process, it still stands out as an unparalleled formula and an ideal metaphor for explaining the spiritual-energetic phenomena—Holy Baptism, Holy Spirit reception, and divinization (whole-bodily en-Light-enment)—that spontaneously accompany the foundational practice of true Christianity: the Eucharist, or Holy Communion.

This Ohm's Law-Eucharist correlation, which I call the "Electrical Spiritual Paradigm," equates Holy (or Divine) Communion with "plugged-in presence," reception of the Holy Spirit with "pulled-down power," and self-surrender with "perfect poverty." In electrical terms, plugged-in presence is *voltage*, pulled-down power is *amperage*, and perfect poverty is *ohms* (relative absence of resistance). If this seems intimidating, ungraspable or too abstract, relax; it will all become clear as you continue through the book, which explains the analogy from multiple perspectives. Once you grasp the Electrical Spiritual Paradigm, you'll marvel at its simplicity and elegance. More importantly, you'll understand—from a scientific-energetic perspective—how to connect to the Divine and channel its electrical-like Power, the Holy Spirit.

The great thing about Ohm's Law and spiritual energy is that a spiritual disciple doesn't have to wait for science to prove they correlate; he can prove it to himself in his own "laboratory," his own bodymind. And based on my own spiritual experience, Ohm's Law (or a modified version of it) does indeed hold true relative to genuine Christian spirituality. Moreover, once a disciple *spiritually* realizes, or conducts and feels, the electrical-like nature of Spirit-energy, he can use this realization as a springboard to radically intuiting, and perhaps ultimately achieving, the *summum bonum* of human existence: God-Realization, eternal abidance in Heaven, the Divine Domain.

Electrical Christianity and the Esoteric Tradition

Even though I wrote this book in a matter of months, it has really been forty years in the making, and represents the culmination of my spiritual experience and thinking. Since graduating from the University of California, San Diego in 1973, I have dedicated myself to the search for spiritual Truth. As an esoteric eclectic, I have devoted myself to both the theory and practice of the foremost spiritual traditions—Theravada, Zen, and Tibetan Buddhism; Hindu Raja Yoga, Advaita Vedanta, and Kashmir Shaivism; Daism (the teachings of Adi Da); and Christian mysticism—and my expertise in these teachings and insights into the relationship between electricity and spirituality has enabled me to originate my Electrical Spiritual Paradigm and integrate it with the preeminent spiritual traditions. Although my main focus in *Electrical Christianity* is the relationship between Christian spirituality and electricity, I also consider other spiritual traditions in order to clarify and reinforce my thesis.

Although my chief aim in this book is to explicate the relationship between electricity and Christian spirituality, my consideration of Christianity isn't limited to this correlative analysis. I also consider it from a general mystical perspective. And because my exposition of the subject is radical and groundbreaking, it can be described as "electrical" even apart from the subject of electricity relative to spiritual energy. Consequently, students of the esoteric tradition will find fertile, and controversial, new ground in this book.

Integral Psychology, Politics, and Sociology

In the final three chapters of the book, I turn my focus to psychology, politics, and sociology relative to Electrical Christianity. In Chapter Thirteen, *Electrical Psychology, Electrical Spirituality*, I present my embryonic vision of "integral" psychology. Students of Ken Wilber, the renowned integralist and author of *Integral Psychology,* will quickly notice that my vision of integral psychology differs markedly from his. In

Chapter Fourteen, *The Spiritual Politics of Jesus*, I deduce Jesus' politics from his actions in the Bible and extrapolate what he would do on a political level if he were now alive and preaching his Gospel. I also present my own political philosophy, which derives principally from my in-depth study of Karl Marx's Marxism and Ayn Rand's Objectivism; and I critique Ken Wilber's "integral politics," which I find less than "integral." In Chapter Fifteen, *Christianity in the Aquarian Age*, I apply my degree in sociology and background as a professional astrologer to analyze the effects of the Earth's shift from Pisces into Aquarius on both Christianity and society in general, and I then present my vision for a *true* [New] Aquarian Age.

Electrical Jesus and a Radical Disciple

Jesus Christ was an electrical individual, a revolutionary in the truest and best sense of the word. He was crucified because he was perceived as a threat to the political and religious establishment of his time. Jesus had no interest in political correctness and no interest in a Dale Carnegie approach of winning friends and influencing people. His overriding interest was in saving souls, in providing the masses with a Way to the Kingdom of Heaven, which isn't of this world. And because nothing in this world is divine or sacred, Jesus mocked established convention on every level, which led to his crucifixion.

In this book, I follow in Jesus' footsteps and make no attempt to placate conventional minds or respect establishment ideals. I present the Truth as I see it, irrespective of the people who might take offense with my radical and irreverent points of view. Although my polemic is sure to cast me as a polarizing figure and cost me readership, my commitment to truth exceeds my desire for book sales. Hence, my response to the fact that many readers will find some of my points of view "extreme" and objectionable is: so be it.

A Brief Summary of This Book

My objective in this book is fivefold: First, to explicate the relationship between electricity and spiritual energy by correlating the essential factors of a basic electrical circuit with those of true, or mystical, Christian spirituality; second, to detail the Plugged-in Presence (or true Holy Communion) method that a disciple can implement in order to realize the correlation between electricity and spiritual energy; third, to point the disciple to the ultimate attainment—God-Realization—that the practice of Electrical Christian spirituality (essentially the Plugged-in Presence, or true Holy Communion, method), leads to and culminates in; fourth, to consider the political and social action in which Jesus might engage if he were incarnate now, in this dark or "late-time" epoch; and fifth, to present an integral New Age vision for a world in dire straits.

Because I believe that the best way to study Christian mysticism (or Christian yoga) is in conjunction with other mystical (or yogic) traditions, I have provided an eclectic spiritual reading list in the Appendix. Though studying esoteric spiritual mysticism is a noble enterprise, the noblest of all is practicing it. Thus, it is my hope is that this book will not only inspire people to practice Electrical (or Spirit-full) Christianity, but also provide them with detailed instructions on how to contact, channel, and unite with the Divine Being, the Living God.

Notes to the Reader

In addition to the term "Plugged-in Presence," I also use the terms "Spirit Communion" and "Divine Communion" interchangeably with "Holy Communion." Holy Communion is about plugging one's consciousness into the Holy Spirit; hence, both "Plugged-in Presence" and "Spirit Communion" are apropos synonyms. The term "Divine Communion" is also a fine synonym, because the term "Divine" refers to the two "vines" of Ultimate Reality—Soul (or Consciousness) and Spirit (or Light-energy), and the act of communion pertains to the disciple's *yogic* attempt to unite these within himself.

I also use a number of synonyms for "Holy Spirit," including some that are common in Christianity, some that derive from other spiritual traditions, and some that are my own creation. Synonyms that I use include, but are not limited to: Pulled-down Power, Blessing Power, Grace, Benediction, Help, Redeemer, Divine Power, Divine Energy, Light-energy, Bliss-current, *Sambhogakaya*, Spirit-power, Spirit-current, Spirit, and *Shakti*. (When "*Shakti*" is uncapitalized, it refers to energy that is less than Divine.)

This book is composed in a question-and-answer format, with the questions and answers derived principally from discussion groups and one-on-one sessions with my students and friends. I have freely edited the questions and answers so as to provide readers with the most enlightening information and instruction. To this end, I have interjected into this book some material from my previous book, *Beyond the Power of Now: A Guide to, and Beyond, Eckhart Tolle's Teachings*. Hence, readers of my Tolle text will notice some familiar bits and pieces in *Electrical Christianity*.

One of the toughest tasks in writing this book was deciding which terms to capitalize and when. For example, a term such as "Power" might merit capitalization in one context but not another. The calls were often subjective, and I'll doubtless revise some of them in further editions.

I use masculine words or pronouns throughout the text, but they should of course be understood in a neutral sense. From a spiritual perspective, distinctions between the sexes are unimportant.

CHAPTER ONE

The "Electrical" Eucharist (The Radical Essence of Jesus' Teachings)

The Crux of Christianity

What does it mean to be a Christian?

Being a true Christian isn't about believing in Jesus; it's about realizing your Christ (or Buddha, or Self)-nature. It's about duplicating Jesus' realization that "I and the Father are One," and the way to do this is by practicing the spiritual discipline that Jesus himself recommends: the Eucharist—the sacrament, or act, of Holy Communion.

At the Last Supper, the last meal he shared with his disciples, Jesus implicitly describes the spiritual discipline that leads to the Kingdom of Heaven (or Christ-consciousness). And this discipline, the Eucharist, is the very essence of not only Christianity but all great mystical (or yogic) traditions.

Our series of discussions will focus on fully explicating the Eucharistic practice of Holy Communion that Jesus alluded to at the Last Supper. We will consider the electrical mechanics of the Eucharistic discipline and the mystical process of becoming Christ-like that the practice of Eucharistic spirituality engenders.

◊ ◊ ◊

So you're saying that Christianity can be reduced to the Eucharist?

Yes, if the Eucharist is properly understood. And I'm not the only one who makes this claim. As the renowned nineteenth-century mystic and occultist Eliphas Levi succinctly put it, "The whole of Christianity is the Eucharist." In other words, if you can understand what the Eucharist is really about, you will also understand what being a true, or Spirit-full, Christian is really about.

The Eucharist is the sacrament, or act, of Holy (or Divine) Communion in its entirety; in other words, the holy (or spiritually holistic) act of connecting to the Divine Source (or Presence) and channeling, or receiving, its Grace (or Blessing Power), in the form of Light-energy. The word "Eucharist," derived from Greek, means "thankfulness" (within the context of communion), and a true devotee of the Divine is always grateful for receiving God's Grace.

Although the Eucharist is the essential component of true, or mystical, Christian spirituality, I contend that it has never been adequately explicated or elaborated upon. My aim as a mystic-philosopher and writer-teacher is to remedy this exegetical deficiency, and to this end, I analogize Eucharistic spirituality to an electrical circuit. I use Ohm's Law to explain the Eucharist, transforming it, in effect, into what I call the "Electrical Eucharist."

Can you explain how to practice the Electrical Eucharist? I really want to practice Holy Communion, but I don't know how.

I think the best way to answer your question is to first explain the basic practice of Holy Communion, and then to elaborate on the explanation via the Electrical Eucharist paradigm. But before

I begin my explanation of Holy Communion, I want to make an important point: Although technical instructions can point the way to the Divine Connection, until you are baptized, or *initiated*, by the Holy One, and receive His Spirit-power, or *Grace*, you cannot practice true Holy Communion—Spirit-infused contemplation of the Divine. Technical instructions for connecting to the Divine pertain mainly to the act of *putting yourself in psycho-physical position to receive* the Benediction, the descent of Divine Power. Once you receive this Divine Blessing Power, this Love-Bliss from above, then instead of you meditating, God, via His *Shakti*, or Spirit-power, meditates you. You rest in the descending Spirit-current, Light-energy from on high, and simply allow it to irradiate, or divinize, your bodymind.

Now that I've prefaced my answer to your question by disclosing the limitations of technical spiritual instructions, I can answer your question. Holy Communion is a synonym for *conscious* relationship, or at-one-ment, with God, *as Spirit;* therefore, the practice of Holy Communion is simply the discipline of conscious relationship, or at-one-ment, with the Holy Spirit. For a man to awaken as a Son who is one with the Father, he must permanently unite his consciousness (or soul) with Spirit-power, Divine Light-energy from above. The fundamental technique for establishing this holy relationship can be summarized as follows:

> Sit upright in a chair with your palms resting on your thighs (or assume a yogic meditation posture on the floor). From your seated position, be whole-bodily present to the empty space in front of you. In other words, consciously inhabit, or "feeling-occupy," your body, and as the whole body, be present to, or pressing against and gazing into, empty space (the void)—which will become shining Presence (the luminous Void) once your connection to it is strong enough to pull down Divine Power, Light-energy from above. To help you

inhabit your body, randomly focus your attention on your hands and "third-eye" area (between, and just above, your brows). Every time, and as soon as, you notice your mind wandering or you feel yourself retracting from the position of being directly present (or in relationship) to the empty space in front of you, simply reassume the whole-bodily asana, or posture, of being present to space. To intensify your efforts to connect to, and stay connected to, space, you can use a verbal enquiry in the form of a question. For example, you can randomly ask yourself: "Avoiding relationship?" This type of self-questioning will focus your attention on your activity of avoiding relationship and instigate your return to the state of connectedness. Alternatively, you can simply pray, intently (and repeatedly, if necessary) asking God to bless you (with His Grace, or Spirit-power). Earnest, focused prayer naturally establishes a disciple in right relationship, which leads to empowered Holy Communion.

When your connection to empty space is sufficiently stable, or "locked-in," it generates conscious force, felt as a palpable energetic pressure. If you utterly yield to this pressure (while maintaining your whole-bodily posture of relationship, or at-one-ment), the Spirit-current, Light-energy from above, can pour into you. When it does, you can either maintain your focused attention on the void (now the luminous Void-Presence), or partially or totally relax it. When the Spirit powerfully "touches" you, the Void-Presence no longer needs reliance. The first time the Spirit touches, or flows into, you is called baptism, or initiation. When, after years, or lifetimes, of spiritual practice, your immersion in the Spirit, the Light-current, becomes constant, then you spontaneously awaken as a Christ, a fully en-Light-ened Son (or Daughter) of God.

Now if you consider the "mechanics" of the Eucharistic Act— connecting to (or plugging into) the Divine Source (or Void-Presence) and then receiving (or conducting) the Power (or Spirit-current) stemming (or emanating) from it—you will notice that it is akin to an electrical circuit. Your bodymind can be likened to an electric lamp, and when you consciously plug it into the Divine Source (or "Socket"), then the Spirit-current flows into and through you, en-Light-ening you with its radiant Energy and "saving" you from your primal "sin," your estrangement from God. Because an electrical circuit is such a wonderful metaphor for the Eucharist, we'll continually return to it in the course of our spiritual discussions.

The Divine Presence and its Divine Power, like fire and its flames, are essentially one. But to become en-Light-ened, you must receive the Divine in the form of Power (Light-energy) emanating from the Presence, hence the emphasis on receiving the Holy Spirit, the en-Light-ening *action* of the Divine. The Divine Presence (the luminous Source or Void) is a marvelous meditation object, but once Its Power begins to pour into you, your relationship to the Divine becomes more a receptive feeling-connection to the Spirit than an active concentration-focus on the Presence. The Bible says to worship God in, and *as*, Spirit; therefore, Divine (or Holy) Communion is essentially Spirit Communion, connecting to the Highest Power, the Holy Spirit, and allowing it to divinize you.

Before we proceed further in our consideration of the Eucharistic method, I want to point out that the fundamental technique I've presented for the practice of Holy, or Divine, Communion is not set in stone. Holy Communion is an art as well as a science; therefore, you can creatively modify my instructions *to a certain degree*. I emphasize "to a certain degree," because communion is simply, and *only*, communion. Thus, "creativity" in the practice of Holy Communion pertains only to your ability to make subtle psycho-physical adjustments that are helpful in enabling you to connect to and "lock in" to the Divine. The creativity I'm talking about can be likened to the adjustments a baseball hitter makes at the plate. Just as a hitter consciously relaxes, breathes deeply, and repositions himself to better enable him to connect his bat to the ball, you likewise can creatively adjust your psycho-physical "positioning" to better enable you to connect to the Divine. In the course of our discussions, we'll consider some adjustments that may help you to establish and maintain a Divine connection.

The Eucharistic Consecration

What is the significance of the bread and wine in the Eucharistic rite?

At his Last Supper, Jesus gives his disciples bread, saying, "This is my body," and wine, saying, "This is my blood." He breaks the bread, implying that man cannot live by bread (or body) alone, that true, or spiritual, sustenance cannot be found through the physical. The message is that man's bodymind isn't intended for sense satisfaction, but rather for sacrificial whole-bodily worship of God. The wine was poured into an empty cup before being given to his disciples, implying that one must empty, or surrender, oneself in order to receive, or to be filled with, the Holy Spirit, the Life-blood of God.

The meaning of the wine is seemingly straightforward, but the breaking of the bread has two meanings: the *physical-sacrificial* one (described above) and a *mystical* one. Thus, when Jesus breaks the bread, he is not only implying that the visible form body must be surrendered (or sacrificed), but that an invisible, or mystical, Truth Body underlies it.

According to most of the Christian sects that accept the mystical meaning of the breaking of bread, when Jesus says, "This is my body," he is referring to a mystical, or invisible, Church, or *Body*, a non-physical communion of all true *believers*. From an esoteric perspective, the Body he is pointing to is the Truth Body (the *Dharmakaya* in Buddhism). The Bible directs us to worship God in Spirit and in Truth; hence, blood refers to the Spirit, and the broken bread to the Truth Body, the invisible, universal God Space, or "Church," in which all true, or Spirit-baptized, *disciples* worship.

Because bread contains yeast and wine is fermented, these two sacramental offerings symbolize the spiritual growth or enzymatic transformation of the disciple. *Transubstantiation* signifies the nth degree of transformation, and the symbolic metamorphosis of bread into the Truth Body (or *Dharmakaya*) and wine into the Holy Spirit (the *Sambhogakaya*, or Bliss Body, in Buddhism) is a reminder for us to surrender, or sacrificially offer ourselves, to the Holy One, so that He, the Master Alchemist, can, via the divinization process, transform us into His likeness.

Baptism by the Spirit

When I attempt to practice Holy Communion, I don't experience the Spirit-energy that you're talking about. Does this mean that I'm not a true Christian?

You can't be a true, or Spirit-connected, Christian—unless you're *baptized*. And the baptism I'm talking about is by the Spirit itself. The Spirit, Holy "Water" from above, literally pours down upon you, infilling your bodymind with intense, flowing Energy. This Energy, or Spirit-power, is your Saving Grace, but until you've been baptized, *initiated* by the Holy One, you can be only a believer, not a true disciple, or faith-full devotee, of the Lord.

If you *religiously* (or *adam*antly) practice the method of Holy Communion that I recommend, and you haven't been baptized after, say, a few months of intense effort (meaning at least two half-hour sessions a day), then you should experiment with the basic concentration/meditation exercises that I'll present in our later discussions.

What do I have to do in order to be baptized?

You have to generate enough conscious force, or "voltage," in your communion practice to "invoke the Deity," to "pull down" the Highest Power. In other words, your "Plugged-in Presence" needs more "push" to transpose into "pulled" (or poured-down) power from above. You get this push by intensifying your concentration, by single-pointedly focusing your attention on the enactment of the Eucharist. In the Sermon on the Mount, Jesus emphasizes this when he says, "If thine eye [consciousness] be single, thy whole body will be filled with Light [from above]."

The greatest aid to generating conscious force is the practice of celibacy. Although sexual abstinence isn't fun, if you're serious about spiritual life and find yourself unable to pull down the Highest Power, the Holy Spirit, then you should experiment with celibacy, or at least with significantly reduced sexual activity. The practice of celibacy isn't about morality; it's about energy—spiritual (or Spirit-connecting) energy. When you abstain from sex, your conserved essential life-energy transmutes into subtle spiritual concentrative power, which helps you to lock into the Divine and pull down Light-energy.

Jesus fasted and prayed for forty days. If you're unable to draw down Divine Power, consider imitating his efforts to a degree. For example, your "imitation of Christ" could be a spiritually intensive, weekend-long or several-day retreat in which you eat sparingly and devote yourself to nearly nonstop prayer, study, and meditation.

Poverty in the Spirit

After the Holy Spirit enters you, what should your spiritual practice be?

When the Spirit "touches" you, you should yield to its invasive pressure by relaxing your body and letting go of your mind. Be as if dead: empty and effortless. This holding on to nothing in the face of Spirit's intrusion is the true meaning of "poverty in the Spirit." The pressure of the Spirit-current sensitizes you to your resistance, enabling you to palpably feel it. And when you feel it, the only intelligent response is to release it and let the Spirit-current move unimpeded through your bodymind, divinizing, or en-Light-ening, you.

When Jesus says, "The meek shall inherit the Earth," he seemingly implies that those who practice poverty in the Spirit, by virtue of the Blessing Power they receive and radiate, will inevitably reign supreme because their selfless purity will be the Saving Grace that rescues humanity from its ego-crazed self-destruction. There is much that can be said about the implications of Jesus' controversial statement, and we'll consider this matter in some depth later.

The Dialectical Eucharist

Can you explain how to integrate the practice of presence with the practice of poverty?

The practices of presence and poverty constitute a dialectic, with presence (or relationship) as the *thesis*, absence (or inner emptiness) as the *antithesis*, and the descent of the Holy Spirit as the *synthesis*. In other words, the pressure of your conscious presence (or relational force) instigates your self-emptying (or surrendering), which "produces," or pulls down, the Spirit, which deifies you, transforming you into a Self-realized, or Christ-like, being.

In engendering the descent of the Spirit, the two dialectical practices of presence (or relationship) and poverty (or absence) give birth to a third, synthesizing practice: the practice of *power*. The practice of presence is about *connecting*; the practice of poverty is about *surrendering*; and the practice of power, which integrates the practices of presence and poverty, is about *receiving*.

The practice of receiving the Holy Spirit *synthesizes* the practices of presence and poverty by, in effect, *mediating* them. Thus, instead of full attention being focused on either the act of being present or the act of being self-empty, the act of receiving, or *conducting*, the Spirit-current involves the artful integration of both these gestures. It involves the *letting go* of psychical content while simultaneously *holding on* to the context of connectedness. In order to instigate the drawing-down of Divine Power, the Holy Spirit, the disciple must sometimes emphasize the "pole of presence" (or relationship), and at other times the "pole of poverty" (or self-emptying). But when the descent of Light-energy is intense, the disciple can dispense with the dialectical spiritual practices (of presence and absence) and effortlessly rest in the Bliss (or Blessing)-current from above.

Ohm's Law and the Eucharist

The dialectical spiritual practice that you're describing does seem to mirror an electrical circuit, with the Spirit-current representing the amperage-like resolution of voltage-like conscious force and ohms-like reduced resistance. But how can you be sure that Ohm's Law applies to spirituality?

No one can prove (or disprove) that Ohm's Law applies to Spirit-conductivity. But based on my own spiritual experiences, it is obvious to me that Ohm's Law, or some approximate variation of it, applies to Eucharistic spirituality. Consequently, even if Ohm's Law does not exactly hold true for the practice of Holy Spirit communion and conductivity, it still provides a nonpareil metaphor for understanding the mechanics of the Eucharist.

For those of you unfamiliar with Ohm's Law, it states that "the strength or intensity of an unvarying electric current is directly proportional to the electromotive force and inversely proportional to the resistance in a circuit." Ohm's Law—where V = voltage (electromotive force), I = amperage (intensity of current), and R = ohms (units of resistance)—can be summarized in three formulas:

$$V = IR \;\; ; \;\; I = \frac{V}{R} \;\; ; \;\; R = \frac{V}{I}$$

(Note: Any form of the Ohm's Law equation can be derived from the other two via simple algebra.)

Translating Ohm's Law into a Eucharistic formula is simple. All we have to do is to substitute communion, or connected consciousness (or consciousness-force), for voltage; spiritual energy (or intensity of the Spirit-current) for amperage; and ego-resistance (or degree of resistance to the Spirit-current) for ohms. Therefore, the Electrical Eucharistic formula—where C = communion, or connected consciousness (or consciousness-force); I = spiritual energy (or intensity of the Spirit-current); and R = ego-resistance (or degree of resistance to the Spirit-current)—can, like Ohm's Law, be summarized in three formulas:

$$C = IR \; ; \; I = \frac{C}{R} \; ; \; R = \frac{C}{I}$$

(Note: As with Ohm's Law, any of these equations can be derived from the other two via simple algebra.)

Can you simplify and summarize the Ohm's Law / Eucharist analogy?

Yes. The Holy Spirit is the electric current (amperage); Holy Communion is the electromotive force (voltage); and ego-resistance is the resistance to the flow of the current (ohms). Ohm's Law applied to Eucharistic spirituality tells us that the intensity of the Holy Spirit-current is directly proportional to one's Holy Communal (or relational) force and inversely proportional to one's ego-resistance to the inflowing Holy Spirit-current. Once you've been baptized by the Holy Spirit, you'll be able to palpably and viscerally experience the seeming reality of Ohm's Law in Eucharistic spirituality.

Ohm's Law is a cool formula for considering the Eucharist, the practice of Holy Communion and Holy Spirit reception. And in our further discussions on Eucharistic spirituality, we'll use the Ohm's Law formula to delve more deeply into the spiritual en-Light-enment process. But before we continue further in this vein, it will be helpful to first consider Christianity's greatest mystery, the Trinity.

CHAPTER TWO

The Holy Trinity (The Triadic "Structure" of Reality)

Understanding the Trinity

No one I've read or talked to seems to understand the Trinity. Do you?

Y ou can judge for yourself how deeply I understand it. But I do want to say that if I hadn't studied and practiced Hindu Kashmir Shaivism, Tibetan Buddhist Dzogchen, and Daism, I wouldn't understand the Trinity to the extent that I do. These spiritual traditions, like Christianity, are trinitarian, and they provided me with the mystico-philosophical insights that I needed to grasp the triadic nature of Reality.

I am a big proponent of trinitarian spirituality, which is why I am so attracted to Christian mysticism. But Christian mysticism can be difficult to deeply understand if one doesn't consider it in the light of other great trinitarian teachings.

Here's how I view the Christian Trinity. The Father, the *Divine* Being-Consciousness, is omni*present* and omni*potent*; in other words, all-pervading Presence (or radiant Space) and Power (or Spirit-energy). The Son, the disciple's Self (or Buddha)-nature, is the same Presence as the Father's, but the disciple cannot realize his True nature as the Son (or Christ, or Self, or Buddha) until the Father's Power (or Spirit-energy) blesses him to the degree of full en-Light-enment. The Holy Spirit is the Father's *dynamic* Power, or Light-energy. It is deemed a separate or unique

Person or Body to differentiate it from the Father's *static* nature as Presence (or Source). Ultimately, Reality is a Monad, but this Monad, the all-subsuming, indivisible Supreme Being, can best be comprehended and apprehended when it is approached from a triadic, or trinitarian, perspective.

The Trinity and the Sacred Heart-center

How, exactly, does the Holy Spirit enable you to realize yourself as a Christ, or Son of God?

The Spirit penetrates you, divinizing (or deifying) you with its Light-energy. When the descending Spirit-current cuts the knot in your Sacred Heart-center (just to the right of the center of your chest), illuminating your soul (the composite of psychical seed tendencies, or impulses, that manifests, or "sprouts," as your mind and emotions), then you awaken as a Christ, or Buddha. Your soul (or "seed consciousness") is located in your Sacred Heart-center (Heart-center, for short), and when your Heart-center knot is cut, your divinized soul, now a Divine Soul, or Son, functions as a perfect reflector of the Infinite, ceaselessly radiating Light unto the world.

Are you saying that the mind isn't located in the brain, that it's really located in the Heart-center?

According to Ramana Maharshi (1879-1950), the greatest Hindu guru of the twentieth century, thought-forms exist as psychical seed-tendencies (*samskaras* in Sanskrit) stored in the Heart-center. These seed tendencies sprout, or rise (via a "subtle," or non-physical, channel) to the brain, where they crystallize as thoughts. Thus, the brain is the organ or medium through which the mind functions, but immanent consciousness itself (the soul) is located in the Heart-center. Any disciple who can "ride" the

Spirit-current into the Heart-center and rest in Heart-felt *samadhi* (absorptive engrossment) can confirm Ramana's observations for himself.

The Heart-center is where your soul (or composite of psychical seed-tendencies) is divinized (or penetrated and illumined) by the Holy Spirit (the descending Spirit-current). The individual soul is the son (or daughter) of God, and when it is en-Light-ened by the Holy Spirit, it becomes the Son (or Daughter) of God. The union (or sacred marriage) of the Son with the Holy Spirit (the Blessed Virgin, or *pure* Divine Blessing Power) in the Heart-center results in the disciple's God-realization, his recognition that "I and the Father are one." Consequently, the only way to the Father is through the Son—but the *spiritual* Son does not emerge until the individual son, or soul, is divinized by the Spirit; and the Father cannot be realized until the Son and the Spirit unite in the Sacred Heart-center.

In Catholic theology, "Mystery" is defined as that which is incapable of being grasped apart from "Divine Revelation." In other words, the Mystery of the Trinity, the three-in-one God, cannot be radically "solved" until the Divine Being reveals Himself to the disciple; and this revelation occurs when the Son and the Spirit unite in one's Heart.

The Trinity in Hinduism and Buddhism

What you're saying sounds exactly like the union of Siva and Shakti in Hinduism.

Yes, the Truth of esoteric Christianity virtually mirrors that of India's tantric traditions. According to the tantric traditions, the individual soul (the *jiva*, or contracted *Siva*) cannot recognize himself as *Siva* (the Self, or Son) until *Shakti* (the Holy Spirit) unites with the *jiva* in the Heart-center. And the union of *Siva* and *Shakti* in the Heart-center results in the Self (or Son) realizing its eternal identity with the Divine Being (the Holy Father). Just as *Siva-Shakti* = Sat (Being), Son-Spirit = Father (Being). The way to the Father is through the Son, but the Son cannot emerge as the Son until the son is awakened by the Holy Spirit.

The truth of Tibetan Vajrayana Buddhism also mirrors that of mystical Christianity. In Vajrayana Buddhism, the three bodies, or hypostases—the *Dharmakaya*, *Nirmanakaya*, and *Sambhogakaya*—are analogous to the Father, Son, and Holy Ghost. Thus, Buddhahood (the *Nirmanakaya*'s realization of his eternal identity with the *Dharmakaya*) cannot occur until the *Sambhogakaya*, the Light-energy (or Bliss, or "Blessing") Body, unites with and frees the *nirmanakaya* (the contracted soul) in the Heart-center. Upon this Nirvanic realization, the awakened Buddha (the now en-Light-ened *Nirmanakaya*) realizes the three bodies, or dimensions, of Reality (the *Trikaya*, or "Triple Body") as an indivisible unity.

Radical Nondual Trinitarian Truth

What is the secret to realizing the truth of the Trinity?

The Trinity is the Truth itself, the Absolute in three apparently distinct "phases" that are ultimately one; hence, the three Persons of the Trinity are said to be *consubstantial*, of the same Supreme Substance or Essence. The key to apprehending and comprehending the Trinity is Grace, the Holy Spirit. The Holy Spirit (*Shakti* in Hinduism, and the *Sambhogakaya* in Buddhism) is the "secret ingredient," or "missing link," that enables the son (or self) to become the Son (or Self) and realize his identity with the Father (the Divine Being). The fact that Baptism by the Spirit is one of the two cardinal sacraments of the Church (the Eucharist is the other) informs us that without the descent of Divine Power, salvation (or en-Light-enment) and a radical (or gone-to-the-root) realization of the Trinity (Triune Reality) are not possible.

I'm still not clear on the Father, the Divine Being, and the nature of His relationship to the Son. Can you elaborate on it?

The Divine Being is infinite, all-pervading Consciousness (or Awareness), eternally shining as radiant Presence-Power. Because the Divine Being is infinite and all-pervading, He can never be reduced to a finite, cognizable object or "Other" that the mind can grasp. Because the Holy One cannot be found through the mind, He is sometimes referred to as the "Hidden God." But when the son (or soul), by virtue of Grace, awakens as the Son (or Soul, or Self), he spontaneously realizes that, as the Seer, the nondual Subject, his own *Beingness* (or divine existence as radiant Presence-Power) is coessential with that of the Divine Being, the Father. Hence, for the disciple, the way to the Father is through the Son.

The Divine Presence-Power is God's effulgence, His Splendor and Glory. When this Splendor is *spiritually* contemplated as static, eternal, all-pervading Light (the timeless Now), then we speak of the Supernal Presence; when this radiance is channeled as dynamic Light-energy, which the disciple draws down, then we speak of Supernal Power. But God's splendorous and glorious Presence-Power is only His *objective* side. For God to be fully realized, His *subjective* (*or non-objective*) side must also be realized. God's subjective side is Consciousness (or Awareness). But Consciousness (or Awareness) can never see or know Itself directly as an Object or "Other"; it can only behold Itself in its own radiance or Light. And for this to happen, the Light-energy from above must pierce the disciple's Heart-knot and unite with his soul (his contracted, or "dark," individual consciousness). The consummation of this Divine Union of Light-energy and consciousness in the disciple's Sacred Heart-center awakens him to his True nature as en-Light-ened Consciousness (or Conscious Light). The Father *is* this Conscious Light, and the Son (the en-Light-ened son) is a perfect human manifestation of the Father, a God-man who unobstructedly reflects, or radiates, His Conscious Light, His Divinity.

Upon his awakening, the Son realizes that Consciousness (or Awareness), his own True nature, is coextensive and coessential with the Divine Presence-Power, which he previously contemplated as a great Object apart from himself. He recognizes himself as consubstantial with the Virgin Mother (the Holy Spirit, or pure Light-energy) and the Ineffable Father (the unknowable Divine Being), and thus the Trinity reveals itself to him as a great Unity, a single indivisible Reality or Truth Body.

Can you simplify and summarize what you've just said?

Yes. The subject (the son, or soul, or individual consciousness) must consciously become one with the Object (the Holy Spirit, or Light-energy) in order to recognize himself as the Subject (the Son, or Self, or Consciousness) who *is* always already one with the Object. The ever-united Subject-Object is the Divine Being (the Father), and the en-Light-ened Son knows that "I and the Father are One."

What you're saying here is way beyond me, but I'm sure it would be construed as heresy by the Orthodox Church.

Yes, it would be considered the height of apostasy, punishable by death just a few short centuries ago. When a great Christian mystic, such as Meister Eckhart (1260-1327), alluded to his own

Christ (or Son)-like identity and realization, he was risking torture and a gruesome death.

The fact that Christian mystics could not speak openly or write about their radical nondual spiritual realization exclusive of Jesus is a major reason why the Trinity has remained such a mystery in Christianity. Consequently, to more deeply understand the Christian Trinity, it is necessary to study other great trinitarian traditions, particularly Hindu Kashmir Shaivism, Tibetan Buddhist Dzogchen, and Daism.

I know that what I've just said about the Trinity is very esoteric and quite challenging to some here, but hopefully it will be perceived as a breath of fresh intellectual air. Consider it an invitation to deep study and thought that will inspire deep spiritual contemplation.

More light will be shed on the Trinity in our further discussions on Electrical Christianity. But the essential point to remember is this: the Holy Spirit is the "missing link" between the Father and the Son, and only when you "find" this link, through the sacraments of baptism and the Eucharist, can the Trinity become a living Reality for you.

CHAPTER THREE

Holy Baptism (Spirit-Initiation)

Baptism and *Shaktipat*

Can you compare Christian Baptism with Hindu Shaktipat?

The Indian yogic term *Shaktipat* means the "descent of Divine Power." Receiving *Shaktipat* initiation is equivalent to being baptized by the Spirit. John the Baptist initiated disciples the same way a *Shaktipat* guru does. Even though he wasn't a fully enlightened master, a Christ, he was a powerful yogi with the ability to transmit *Shakti* to ripe seekers.

Is a guru necessary for baptism?

It depends on the seeker. Innumerable yogis have awakened to the Spirit without the help of a human intermediary, but the Grace flowing through a master, or even an advanced teacher, can often trigger the Spirit-baptism of a disciple. Empowered spiritual sites, such as holy temples and sacred burial grounds, can also facilitate *initiation*.

Electrical Baptism

What is the best way for a disciple to awaken to the Spirit on his own? I have no interest in searching for a guru.

The spiritual practice that generates the most "voltage," or conscious "push," is what most effectively pulls down the Spirit-current from above. And this practice is the discipline of Holy Relationship (or Communion). Conscious push = relational force, and this relational force instigates the flow of Grace from above. Holy Relationship (or Communion) is simply the practice, or sacred discipline, of religiously, or intensely and devotedly, plugging into the Divine Being (or Source), and receiving, or conducting, *His* Power (or Spirit-energy). Thus, the best way to awaken to the Spirit and receive your initial "Gift from God" is to practice Holy Communion.

Even if you don't want a guru, you should participate in a spiritual prayer/meditation group and/or find a sacred, empowered church or temple to practice in. The spiritual force field generated by a group or provided by a holy temple significantly favors the flow of *Shakti*. In a gross secular environment, it is much more difficult to invoke the descent of the Divine. Even advanced disciples benefit from the free flow of Grace available in a sacred milieu.

What does it feel like when the Spirit initiates you?

It varies according to one's karma. In some cases, the "touch" from above is light; in other cases, it is intense, as the Divine Power seems to crash down on the disciple. Usually, it is felt as a distinct pressure in the head, particularly in the third-eye area. One's head and/or body may jerk or shake in response to the Spirit's invasion.

Once you awaken to the Spirit, you can rest in its Power and mystically (or yogically) *contemplate* the Divine. In Christian mysticism, this stage of contemplation is termed *infused contemplation.* Prior to infused contemplation, the disciple practices *acquired contemplation,* prayer and meditation exercises that help him to establish a connection to the Divine. Thomas Keating, a Trappist monk who has championed the resurgence of the contemplative dimension of the Gospel, calls these two stages of contemplation *centering prayer* and *contemplative prayer*. Keating's book *Open Mind, Open Heart*, which I strongly recommend, is an excellent introductory text to the Christian contemplative tradition.

You say that the Eucharist is the "whole of Christianity," but now you are emphasizing baptism. Can you clarify the relationship between the Eucharist and baptism?

In *The Foundations* of *Mysticism*, author Bernard McGinn, the foremost scholar of Western Christian mysticism, identifies baptism as "foundation" and Eucharist as "crown" relative to the teachings of Jesus. In other words, according to McGinn, the "rock" that true Christianity is built on is baptism. For unless you are baptized by (or in) the Spirit, the Eucharist has no real significance. A good analogy is an electric lamp. Ohm's Law (analogous to the Eucharist) can be said to represent the lamp's functioning circuitry, the physics that enables it to shine light. But unless the lamp receives power from a source (analogous to baptism and Spirit-reception), it can't be turned on, and Ohm's Law will have no significance relative to it.

As long as you are practicing *acquired contemplation* (or *centering prayer/meditation*), you haven't received Power from the Source; hence the "electrical" (or Spirit-energized) Eucharist remains just an abstraction to you. But once you've been baptized and have graduated to the practice of *infused contemplation* (*contemplative prayer*, or *empowered meditation*), then the Eucharist—the sacrament of becoming Christ-like by virtue of Grace— concretely represents the whole of Christianity to you.

Baptism by Water and Fire

What is the significance of being baptized in water?

Water baptism symbolizes the washing away of sin through a new life to be lived in the Spirit. But, of course, in mainstream churches, baptism is merely ceremonial, and the "initiated" are not really *initiated*. Because water is the universal solvent, it is the perfect symbol for the cleansing from original, or primal, sin, separation from God. But symbolic baptism can't save you from your *primal sin* of separation; only baptism in (or by) the Spirit can.

Why is the Spirit sometimes referred to as the Baptist Fire?

Our sins are not just "washed away" by the Spirit; they are also "fried" in the Baptist Fire, the flaming heat of the Light-energy from above. God is an all-consuming Fire, and unless you submit to His white-hot Energy, and are transformed into a living Flame, a single, radiant Intensity, you cannot become spiritually en-Light-ened. Ultimately, the Spirit is experienced as a Bliss-current—but before you can rest in the Ambrosia from above, you must first suffer the heat of the purgatorial Fire.

Spirit-baptism can begin as a light and pleasant experience, a "touch" from above. But at some point, if your spiritual life is to evolve into a truly Spirit-full one, you must experience the fiery, violent action of the Spirit. Matthew 11:12 says, "The Kingdom of Heaven suffers violence, and the violent take it by force." This was true in the days of John the Baptist, and it is true today. The force of your Plugged-in Presence must pull down the Highest Power, the Upper Force, and this Force, or Spirit-power, must "violently," or intensely and energetically, purify your bodymind, transforming you into a fit vehicle for the Divine.

Why doesn't the Church teach this?

We live in a dumbed-down, de-estericized society, created and perpetuated by both the State (the leviathan government) and the Church (the conventional religious establishment). The State (via its army of brain-dead bureaucrats and secular educators) preaches *statism*, servitude to the fascist, neo-Marxist, Mafia-like government; and the Church (via its collection of depthless pulpiteers masquerading as "holy men") preaches *churchianity*, blind belief in exoteric Christian dogma. Just as the State, through public schools, including universities, fails to teach *individualism*, the principle of personal and economic liberty espoused in the U.S. Constitution, likewise, the Church neglects to teach *spirituality*, the principles of Spirit baptism and Spirit communion.

It sounds like the Matrix.

Exactly. The State, Corporate America, and the Mainstream Media (which obediently pushes the messages of the State and Corporate America) have, in a neo-Orwellian manner, combined to create a Matrix of sorts, a sociocultural zeitgeist that, in effect, puts a ceiling on individual freedom, intellectual inquiry, and spiritual verticality. The Church creates its own form of the Matrix, brainwashing its "sheep" with an exoteric, anti-mystical, ultra-moralistic version of real Christianity.

So we need to take the red pill, not the blue.

Take the *Shakti* pill, and wash it down with Holy Water from above. For if you want to ascend above the Matrix, you must first allow the Holy Spirit to crash down through it, so it can liberate you, allowing you, like the phoenix, to rise above the "Network of Madness."

CHAPTER FOUR

Holy Communion (Plugged-in Presence)

Communion = Presence + Oneness

One of the books I've recently read, The Power of Now, *by Eckhart Tolle, emphasizes the practice of presence as the key to spiritual enlightenment. But this book doesn't even mention the Holy Spirit, which you emphasize. What do you have to say about this?*

I have actually written a book—*Beyond the Power of Now: A Guide to, and Beyond, Eckhart Tolle's Teachings*—that answers your very question in extensive detail. For now, I have three summary responses to your question.

First, *real* spirituality isn't about the practice of *mere* presence; it's about the practice of *plugged-in* presence. Plugged-in presence means presence + oneness. Presence + oneness = communion, or relationship, or unity consciousness, or conscious at-one-ment. The pop New Age gurus, like Tolle, emphasize *mere* presence because the idea of connecting to and channeling Divine Power is anathema to their emphasis on *personal* presence and power.

Second, as you point out, *The Power of Now* has nothing to say about the Power of the Now, the Holy Spirit. The only en-Lightening Power that stems, or emanates, from the Now, timeless Presence, is Spirit-power, the Holy Spirit. Yet, Tolle, shockingly, never mentions this Spirit-power, even when he discusses Jesus' teachings. How can Tolle's book legitimately bear the subtitle *A*

Guide to Spiritual Enlightenment when he fails to even broach the subject of Spirit and its role as en-Light-ening agent?

Third, we live in a plastic, pop, celebrity-driven culture. Hence, superficial pop gurus, like Tolle, thanks to big-name media figures like Oprah, who push them, become superstars. They sell millions of books, host shows on PBS, and spread their New Age pabulum around the world. To undiscerning Truthseekers, Eckhart Tolle and his ilk appear to be true gurus, marrying the wisdom of the East with the science of the West. But to the discerning, those steeped in esoteric mystical traditions, they are just snake oil salesmen in drag, peddling insipid, dumbed-down versions of the real wisdom teachings in conjunction with bastardized science. The New Age gurus don't talk about Spirit's role in the en-Light-enment process because they lack expertise on the subject and know that by emphasizing simplistic, popular themes such as self-awareness, living in the moment, and saving the planet, they can make a mint.

Radical Obedience: Non-Avoidance of God

How does plugged-in presence differ from just presence?

If you turn on a lamp that isn't plugged in, nothing happens. Similarly, your mere awareness, or presence, will lack conscious-relational force if it's not connected to the Divine Source (or Presence). Plugged-in presence = communion, or conscious relationship. In every moment, you sin by avoiding relationship with the Divine. In other words, the root sin of humans is to "fall" (or retract) from Grace, God's Holy Spirit, or Blessing Power. You can *atone* for your sinful activity of retracting from the Divine by assuming, or reassuming, the holistic *asana* (or holy psycho-physical "posture") of *at-one*-ment with the Holy One.

◊ ◊ ◊

So we are bad boys and girls who constantly ignore God?

Yes. Ignorance (of God) is the primal human sin. The human ego, from a psycho-spiritual perspective, is simply the moment-to-moment activity of ignoring, or avoiding, at-one-ment with the Spirit. A Christian mystic takes three sacred vows: *obedience*, *chastity*, and *poverty*. Obedience simply means being present to and at-one with the Spirit. Radical (or gone-to-the-root) obedience means *radical under-standing*, that is, "standing" (or being directly present) *under* the Spirit, and allowing its Power to pour down upon you. *The Secret Book of John*, the foremost Christian Gnostic text, beautifully summarizes radical obedience (or "under-standing") thus: "[He] stood in the Spirit's presence, and it was poured upon him."

Chastity, the second sacred vow, pertains to living, or abiding, in the poured-down Spirit, the unborn, pure, or "virgin," Light-energy from above. Whenever you allow the Blessed Virgin to grace you with her Benediction, you *are* a pure, or chaste, soul. But the moment you retract from the Light, you *become* impure, a "sinner."

Poverty simply means self-emptying, letting go of all clinging and grasping. In the context of being present to the Spirit, you become an empty vessel, a holy chalice ready to be filled with Light-energy, the ambrosial Influx from above.

The three sacred vows succinctly summarize what real spirituality, real mysticism, real Christianity is all about. You practice Holy Communion (or radical *obedience*) by plugging into the Spirit, and you allow the Spirit to bless you (with its *chaste* Light) by utterly emptying (or *impoverishing*) yourself.

Break on Through (to the Other Side)

The idea of obedience to an invisible Being is not my idea of enlightenment. I'm a non-conformist, and I want to be free, not tethered to a Deity.

I've got bad news for you: There is nothing you can *do* to free yourself. Everything *you* do entails karma, and thus bondage on one level or another. If you really want to be a radical non-conformist, "doing" what less than one in a thousand people is doing, then become a devotee of the Divine. The other 999 out of 1,000 imagine themselves as non-conformists, doing their own thing, but in reality, they are brainwashed conformists, buying into the myth of soul independence. If you want to be a true free soul, then you will turn to the Holy One and allow Him, via his *Shakti*, to untie your knots of bondage. Then, instead of swimming in the tiny "fishbowl" of your form-grasping mind, playing the same programmed "tapes" over and over, you will be floating in the infinite ocean of the *formless* One Mind, the all-pervading, luminous Void-Awareness. You have two choices: You can remain a *conformist* and grasp after volitional *formations*, or you can become a *non-conformist* and commune with the *Formless* One.

You said there is nothing we can do to free ourselves, but isn't practicing Holy Communion a volitional act?

Holy Communion isn't you doing something to free yourself; it is only you "positioning" yourself so as to allow the Holy One, via His Spirit Power, to free, or save, you.

But don't we need to intensely plug into the Divine Source? Don't we need to generate sufficient conscious force to awaken and pull down the Spirit?

Consciously "positioning" yourself naturally generates *all* the conscious force or "voltage" you need to pull down the Spirit. Consciously "positioning" yourself is simply assuming, or attempting to assume, the holistic *asana*, or whole-bodily "posture," of *relationship*. Relationship = presence + oneness. When relationship is direct and unqualified, it generates maximal conscious force. Hence, relationship, which is a synonym for communion, spontaneously morphs into empowered Divine (or Holy) Communion once relationship becomes "Divine"—meaning that the "vine" of your consciousness (the Son) directly interfaces with the "vine" of the Spirit (the Virgin Mother).

In response to his fundamental resistance, the avoidance of relationship, a yogi struggles to remain present and plugged in. Hence, from his perspective, it seems as if he must exercise intense conscious effort to cut through his recalcitrant mind-forms. His aim is to penetrate through them, so he can "break on through" to the Other Side: the luminous, "dancing" Void. But in reality, there is nothing to cut through. Simply by assuming the "posture of plugged-in presence," he has already "leapt over" all psychical obstructions to the "Objective Face of Reality." If he simply maintains his position of direct and immediate presence, the Spirit will eventually show its Face. As the great seventh-century Zen master Hui Hai put it, "Straightforwardness is the Holy Place." In other words, when you are in direct, unobstructed relationship to existence, the whole, then you are ready for your face-to-Face "meeting" with the Holy One.

The late '60s rock group Blind Faith—you can check them out at Youtube.com—sang, "I have finally found a way to live in the Presence of the Lord," and another '60s rock group, the Doors (influenced by Aldous Huxley's book *The Doors of Perception*), rhapsodized about "breaking on through (to the Other Side)." In reality, if you simply maintain the *asana* of relationship (or universal communion), you will spontaneously live in the Presence of the Lord and break on through to the Other Side.

The Esoteric Meaning of "Waiting"

Can you cite a parable from the Bible that supports your vision of real spirituality and real Christianity versus Eckhart Tolle's?

Most of the Bible is exoteric, consisting of Jesus' teachings for the general public. But there are parables which make it clear that the practice of presence, or "watching," or "witnessing," will not save you unless the Spirit graces you. I think the best way for me to answer your question is via an excerpt from my book *Beyond the Power of Now*:

> According to Eckhart Tolle, the "esoteric meaning of waiting" is being "present with your whole being." "Something could happen in any moment," says Tolle, "and if you are not absolutely awake, absolutely still, you will miss it." This "alert presence," Tolle tells us, "is the kind of waiting Jesus talks about," and in that state, Tolle says, "all your attention is in the Now."

> To illustrate the "esoteric" meaning of waiting, Tolle cites, from the Bible, the *parable of the wise and foolish virgins* (Matthew 25). Here's Tolle's interpretation of it:

> Jesus speaks of the five careless (unconscious) women who do not have enough oil (consciousness) to keep their lamps burning (stay present) and so miss the bridegroom (the Now) and don't get to the wedding feast

(enlightenment). These five stand in stark contrast to the five wise women who have enough oil (stay conscious).

Is Tolle's interpretation of this parable truly an "esoteric" one? Let me put it this way: If I were a professor of Biblical Studies at Cambridge and he were my student, I'd flunk him. First of all, *oil* does not represent *consciousness* in the Bible; it represents the Holy Spirit. Noted Biblical scholar Stanley M. Horton, in his book *What the Bible Says About the Holy Spirit,* has this to say about the symbolic meaning of oil in the Bible:

Oil clearly represents the anointing of the Spirit. Through-out the Bible oil continues to be an important symbol of the Holy Spirit. It speaks of the real anointing, the "unction from the Holy One" (1 John 2:20) which in the New Testament is extended to every believer.

Second, the *bridegroom* is not the *Now*; it's the Son of Man, and this is clearly stated by Matthew himself. The Son of Man, from an esoteric point of view, is the second Person of the Holy Trinity, the human soul (in the Sacred Heart-center), which, upon uniting with the third Person of the Trinity, the Holy Spirit, awakens to its Sonship, its oneness with the Father, who represents the Now, the timeless divine Presence. If the bridegroom is the Now, as Tolle claims, how could the careless women (actually *virgins*, according to the Bible) miss him? If he is the Now, he would be ever-present, but as Matthew says, "Watch therefore, for you know neither the day nor the hour in which the Son of Man is coming." In other words, the reason we do not know when the Son of Man is coming is that the human soul cannot morph into the Son of Man until the Holy Spirit enters the sacred Heart-center and anoints it with its "oil." Third, Tolle equates the *wedding feast* with enlightenment. There is no wedding feast in this parable; there is only a *wedding*, and this wedding signifies the union of the virgin (or Holy) Spirit and the Son. The Now cannot be fully realized until the Holy union between the virgin Spirit and the Son (who dwells in the Sacred Heart) is consummated, but it is not possible for us to know when our spiritual "wedding" is scheduled.

Here's my interpretation of Matthew 25: The five ignorant *virgins* are *pure* practitioners of presence, but because they lack oil (*Shakti*, the Holy Spirit), they cannot keep their lamps burning (sustain their watching, or witnessing, practice), and so they miss the bridegroom (the Son of Man) and the wedding (the Holy Union), and thus remain unenlightened (unrecognized by the Lord).

If you want to abide in the kingdom of God, the eternal Now, you must, as Jesus says in John 4, "worship God in spirit and truth." If you practice "alert presence," which Tolle equates with "esoteric waiting," you are worshipping God in truth, but if you want to maintain, and ultimately consummate, your connection to the Now, you must also worship God in spirit. In Acts 1:8, Jesus tells us that the power of the Holy Spirit will make us witnesses. Jesus here is informing us that we cannot practice true and sustained watching, or witnessing, until we receive the Holy Spirit, the power of Now. Unfortunately, Tolle never mentions the Holy Spirit and how it pertains to the practice of being present (or bearing witness). Therefore, the "esoteric meaning of waiting" that Tolle provides us with is really an exoteric one. Hence, when Tolle says that "Even the men who wrote the Gospels did not understand the meaning of these parables," it's a case of the pot calling the kettle black, a case of an *exoteric* mystic making a fool of himself by grossly misinterpreting the Gospels.

So the message, which Tolle misses, is that we need to worship God not only in Truth, but in Spirit, too?

Yes. And Tolle doesn't even present the integral, or holistic, way to worship in Truth. Instead of teaching Plugged-in Presence, Holy Communion, he pushes mere, or truncated, presence.

"Medicine" for the "Drunken Monkey"

When I sit down each morning and attempt to practice Holy Communion, my mind wanders endlessly and I do not connect with the Spirit. What should I do to stop my mind from jumping around like a drunken monkey?

Your problem is hardly unique. In fact, it is the same one that every un-en-Light-ened being suffers from, to one degree or another. We are all prodigal sons, wandering souls in self-imposed exile from the Promised Land, the Kingdom of Heaven. The term "soul" is synonymous with "psyche, or "mind," and until you achieve God-union, your mind, or soul, will not be at rest.

The highest, or holiest, thing you can do to combat your restless and resistant mind is to single-pointedly devote yourself to the sacrament of Holy Communion. In *The Bhagavad Gita*, the Hindu Bible, Krishna, the Divine Lord, instructs Arjuna, his devotee, how to conquer his mind and achieve Divine Union. He says to Arjuna, "Set your mind on me and fight." In other words, as soon as you become aware that your mind has wandered, resolutely reassume, or attempt to reassume, the whole-bodily *asana* of direct and immediate relationship. Be organismically present to the empty space in front of you, and as soon as you feel yourself retracting from at-one-ment with it, reestablish your connection.

When the empty space in front of you begins to "dance," when it comes alive as a living Presence, then instead of being present to a mere void, you will be present to the shimmering Void, the shining Presence. When the Power (or en-Light-ening Energy) of this Presence, the Holy Spirit, enters you, then you will periodically experience yourself merging with the Presence. And when, after years, or lifetimes, of spiritual practice, the Power of the Presence severs your Heart-knot, then you will no longer experience yourself as present to Presence; instead, you will be present *as* Presence, *as* Consciousness-Radiance Itself.

So the Holy Spirit is the Elixir that cures the drunken monkey mind?

Exactly. "Sober Intoxication" from above naturally supplants drunken, or toxic, mind-forms from below. Connecting to Spirit, Divine Power, not only is the key to being able to sustain the practice of presence but also the cure for the unruly mind. The Holy Spirit, Light-energy from on high, naturally obstructs the arising of chaotic thought-forms. And Eucharistic Communion is the only "method" that enables a disciple to directly plug into the Spirit. Therefore, a true disciple is really a fundamental "Methodist," one who religiously practices the Method of the Holy Ones: Holy Communion (or Plugged-in Presence).

CHAPTER FIVE

Holy Spirit Reception (Pulled-down Power)

Reception = Presence + Poverty

When the Spirit "touches" us, what should we do? Just yield to its pressure?

You can either passively yield to Spirit's "Invasion" or actively seek to unite with its Energy. In other words, like a vagina, you can allow yourself to be penetrated by the inpouring Power, or, like a phallus, you can seek to penetrate it.

Totally yielding, or emptying yourself, to receive the Spirit is termed *poverty* in Christian mysticism, and seeking to unite with It is referred to as the practice of (plugged-in) *presence*.

From a dialectical perspective, presence is the thesis, poverty is the antithesis, and reception of the Spirit is the *synthesis*. In other words, the pressure of your (plugged-in) presence "awakens" the Spirit, and your self-emptying provides the opening for its descent.

Real spirituality is primarily about the dialectical practices of *presence* and *poverty*, because the synthesis of these two is what enables you to receive, or conduct, Spirit-power. The "art" of spiritual practice is the "skillful means" of integrating the practices of presence and poverty to enable you to receive, or conduct, maximal Spirit-power.

Electrical Spiritual Exercise

Both before and after you experience the descent of Spirit-power, you can, as a spiritual exercise, alternate the practices of presence (or consciousness + oneness) and poverty (or absence). This is tantamount to alternating between increasing voltage (force) and decreasing ohms (resistance) to intensify current flow in an electrical circuit. If you haven't been baptized by the Spirit, you won't experience the Spirit-current, but this practice still will stimulate the movement of energy in your body.

Begin the *electrical spiritual exercise* by being directly present to the void (or to the Spirit, if you have awakened it), and as soon as you feel uncomfortable pressure from your connection, or your attempt to establish a connection, totally let go, allowing the Spirit, if you have awakened it, to penetrate you. Whenever your attempt at letting go (or self-emptying) becomes burdensome, simply revert to the practice of (Plugged-in) Presence. This spiritual exercise is fundamentally the same both prior to and after Baptism by the Spirit, but only after you have been *initiated* by the Holy Spirit can it become a truly *Spirit-full* exercise. Once it becomes a truly Spirit-full exercise, then instead of full attention being focused on either the act of being present or the act of self-emptying, you'll be able to integrate both these gestures into the single act of receiving, or conducting, the Spirit-current. You'll be able to remain tacitly present and connected while simultaneously releasing resistance to the inflow of Power from above.

So we can dispense with the electrical spiritual exercise *once we are rested in the Divine?*

The need for spiritual exercise comes to an end when you achieve *samadhi,* locked-in engrossment in the Divine. Once you are fully absorbed in the Spirit-current, there is no need to practice exclusive presence or poverty, because unimpeded reception represents the synthesis of these two "poles." But as soon as you lose your state of blissful absorption, you need to reinstate the electrical spiritual exercise.

Secondary Spiritual Practices

Is there anything other than the practices of presence and absence that can help a disciple connect to and channel the Higher Power?

Yes, there are *secondary practices*, which are to be implemented in the context of the primary practices of presence and absence. These secondary practices are helpful complements to the primary practices, and you should freely employ them to help you connect to and channel the Holy Spirit. These secondary practices are where "skillful means" come into play. They are forms of individual spiritual expression, and there is no set formula for practicing them. Experiment with them and use them to whatever extent they help your spiritual practice.

The foremost secondary practice to consider is that of *devotion*. Some religions and spiritual traditions consider loving devotion to God a primary spiritual practice, but it isn't, because, in and by itself, it's a practice that depends on mind and emotion rather than on Consciousness and Spirit. Because devotional love depends on human will and effort, it can only be practiced spasmodically. This does not mean that devotion isn't a powerful and effective method; it just means that it is an indirect and secondary one.

Devotional love, ardent feeling-attachment, can help a disciple connect to, and maintain his connection to, the Divine. When a disciple of the Truth becomes a *devotee* of the Lord, it becomes easier for him to lock into the Spirit and allow *It* to en-Light-en him. Devotion facilitates both communion and surrender and, as such, is an ideal complementary practice. Purely gnostic communion can be dry, but devotional communion—communion practiced in conjunction with love and feeling—imbues one's spiritual life with warmth and vitality.

Devotees of the Divine often find that gazing at uplifting religious art (such as statues or pictures of Jesus or Buddha), listening to inspiring spiritual music (such as Pachelbel's *Canon* or Paul Horn's *Inside the Taj Mahal*), or reading from a holy book (such as the Bible or the Bhagavad Gita) can serve as a devotional catalyst. Feel free to use whatever spiritual "enzymes" open your heart and turn your attention to the Lord.

Another very helpful secondary practice is that of *pranayama* (conscious breathing aimed at intensifying the force and flow of one's *prana*, or subtle life-energy). In *Beyond the Power of Now*, I describe the practice of *pranayama* that I recommend—*electrical pranayama*—and its spiritual significance. The description reads as follows:

> I have experimented with virtually every form of yogic *pranayama*, and in my opinion, the most efficacious and natural one is what I call *electrical pranayama*. Here is the practice: After you assume your whole-bodily *asana* of relationship, simply be in direct relationship to your breathing cycle. Direct relationship (awareness + oneness) = maximal consciousness-force (pure consciousness plugged directly into life). And because *pranayama* is simply (and only) *conscious* breathing, the result of combining maximal conscious force—via relationship—with the breath is the most powerful form of *pranayama* possible.

According to Walter Russell (1871–1963), the renowned spiritual polymath, there are just two primary forces in the universe: *charge* and *discharge*. When you consciously breathe in, you effectively charge (or infuse) your organism with *prana*, and when you consciously breathe out, you discharge (or circulate and radiate) *prana*. Charge and discharge are akin to voltage (force) and amperage (flow) in an electrical circuit; therefore, if (in the context of conscious whole-body relationship) you practice full inbreathing (all the way down to your navel) and full outbreathing (utterly emptying your lungs, and your mind, too), you will maximize the force (+) and flow (-) of *prana* in your "body electric."

Pranayama, the conscious exercise of charging and circulating subtle life-energy, is a wonderful discipline that should be practiced by all yogis. But, again, *pranic* energy should not be equated with the Holy Spirit, the divine Spirit-current. Only when your practice of direct and immediate relationship (or true Holy Communion) is full enough and intense enough will you be *initiated* by the Holy Spirit, Mother *Shakti*. How will you differentiate between the Holy Spirit (the Baptist Fire) and *pranic* energy? It's very simple: the Baptist Fire literally crashes down on you. The definition of *Shaktipat* is the "descent of divine Power," and when this *Shakti* (or Holy Fire) pours (or rages) through you, its intensity will rock your body, periodically causing it to jerk or shake with *kriyas*, spontaneous purifying movements.

Life-force contemplation and pranic energy exercises are yoga practices that *you perform*; *Shaktipat* yoga *is performed on you*, by the Deity. All you do is receive the

Benediction, the Grace-full invasion of the inpouring Divine Power. Contemplating your inner energy-field and circulating *prana*, or *chi*, will vitalize and balance your body and help you to silence your mind, but these practices are only preliminaries to receiving the Blessing Power of the Bliss Body, the "body bright."

Devotional love and *electrical pranayama* may be the most important secondary spiritual practices, but they aren't the only ones. For example, the Chinese energy disciplines of *tai chi* and *chi gung* (*qigong*) can also serve as helpful adjuncts to the primary practices. In reality, whatever discipline helps you connect to or conduct the Spirit can be considered a "secondary spiritual practice."

The Song of Songs and the Virgin Mother

Should we think of the Holy Spirit as a lover or as a mother?

In Matthew 1:18, Jesus is described as a "child of the Holy Spirit." In other words, according to the New Testament, Jesus' true mother is the Virgin Spirit. But in the Song of Songs (of Solomon), in the Old Testament, the Spirit is depicted as a bride (or lover) that, after courtship (spiritual practice), marries (or spiritually unites with) the bridegroom (the disciple). Throughout the ages, the Song of Songs has been the favorite parable of Christian mystics who have sought intercourse with the Spirit in lieu of physical sex.

If the Spirit is both our mother and lover, and we are seeking to spiritually penetrate (or "make love" to) her, then, in Freudian terms, we are talking about an Oedipus complex. The question is, how do we resolve this problem? The answer is simple: The Spirit, in reality, is neither mother nor lover; it is simply God's Energy, and we are free to conceive of this Energy in whatever way best serves our spiritual practice. Female and homosexual spiritual practitioners, for instance, are welcome to think of the Energy in male terms.

The fact that the grammatical gender of the word "Spirit" is masculine in Latin (*"Spiritus"*), feminine in Hebrew (*"Ruach HaKodesh"*), and neuter in Greek (*"Pneuma"*) tells us that God's Energy can be thought of as male, female, or neither.

Holy Fire and Grace

In your excerpt from Beyond the Power of Now, *you describe the Holy Spirit as a raging fire that literally crashes down on devotees. Can you elaborate on the function of Spirit as a purifying fire?*

Before a disciple can experience *pure* spiritual Light, he must first experience spiritual Fire, the *purifying* "flames" of the inpouring divine Power. When the Divine contacts you, It does so as an impersonal living Force. This Force "wants" to flow through you and en-Light-en you with Its radiant Energy, but what It encounters in, and *as*, you, is a body of psycho-physical resistance. Before the Light can shine through you, the Fire must first "burn" through your psycho-physical resistance, your karma. This amalgam of resistance(s) that you are includes knots (*chakras*) in your "inner," or subtle-body, energy field, as well as deeply buried or strongly suppressed psychic content. The fiery Energy must burn through these resistances before It can express Itself as pure Light; and this process of being organismically exposed to the divine Fire is termed *purgatory* in Christian mysticism and *tapas* (heat) in Hindu yoga. In India, a perfectly en-Light-ened master is said to be "fully cooked."

Both true Christianity and Hindu Kashmir Shaivism, the acme of Indian yoga, emphasize the importance of the violent action of the Spirit. In Matthew 11:12, which I've referred to before, the

Bible says: "And from the days of John the Baptist until now the kingdom of heaven suffers violence, and the violent take it by force." And in Kashmir Shaivism, the violence of the *Shakti* that a yogi experiences is correlated with his potential for en-Light-enment: the greater the violence, the greater the potential.

So Grace is measured out?

Yes. The more spiritually evolved the disciple is, the greater is his capacity to channel Grace, the downpoured Spirit. If Grace wasn't measured out by God, via His universal Law, then yogis would be fried alive in the divine Fire. The path to the Immeasurable must be gradual, so that one's psycho-physical vehicle can, by degrees, adapt to the Holy Invasion. Although the *Shakti* can seem overwhelmingly intense and violent at times, God never gives you more than you're karmically constituted to handle.

It sounds as if "Grace" is not always Graceful.

Au contraire: Grace is *always* graceful. What's not graceful is your resistance to Its "Work." If you utterly yield to Its Will, Its Power, then even your "painful" psycho-physical experiences will be recognized as a Gift, or Blessing, from above. You must understand that spiritual salvation is not possible without *divinization*, the process of whole-bodily en-Light-enment that *is performed on you by the Spirit.* If you view the fiery action of the Divine in this light, then you will understand that the Benediction is always benign.

The Bible contradicts your statement that Grace is measured out. I just opened to John 3:34, and it reads, "For He whom God has sent speaks the words of God, for God does not give the Spirit by measure."

You have a New King James Version of the Bible. In older King James versions, the verse ends with "God does not give the Spirit by measure *unto Him*" (italics mine). In other words, a *fully* en-Light-ened being, such as Jesus, does receive the Spirit sans measure, but for the rest of us, it is measured out in accordance with our karma and ability to access the Spirit. By practicing Plugged-in Presence, Holy Communion, you maximize your Spirit-conductivity potential.

What about the Dark Night of the Soul?

As the spiritual adept Adi Da (1939-2008) put it, "The dark night of the soul is just Narcissus." In other words, if you relinquish your egoic point of view and depersonalize your psychic pain, your suffering disappears. Darkness is simply the absence of Light, and Narcissus, a metaphor for the ego, is simply the soul's activity of avoiding the Light (and its purifying Fire). Therefore, whenever you experience the "dark night of the soul," recognize it as a reminder to return to the Light and to accept its fiery action as a Blessing.

But I don't experience the Light or Its purifying Fire. I just experience my suffering.

Your suffering is your own psychical activity, which contracts consciousness into successive, limited, and hence "painful," states (of consciousness). You can blunt your suffering to a degree by living integrally and learning how to think positively, but the fact is, there is no desirable state. Every state or condition, whether "positive" or "negative," is a contraction, a "knotting" of consciousness. The only radical (or gone-to-the-root) way out of suffering is through Grace, the Light-energy that outshines the mind and renders the self-contraction temporarily (and eventually permanently) defunct. Every other "solution" is remedial. Consequently, the only radical, or non-remedial, thing you can do regarding your suffering is to intensify your efforts to awaken to the Holy Spirit, so you can receive *Its* Blessing (and Healing) Power.

I feel uncomfortable pressure in my head, particularly in my third-eye area, when I pray or meditate. What do you recommend that I do?

The pressure in your head probably signifies that the Spirit is pressing down on you, trying to pass through your *ajna* (or third-eye) "door." Try consciously relaxing your head region when you meditate. If the pressure increases when you relax, you'll know it's the Spirit opening up, or moving through, the *chakras* in your head. Pressure or tightness in the head and neck area is common when the *Shakti* invades a yogi. This pressure can even cause one's head to jerk and body to shake. These jerking and shaking movements, or *kriyas*, can continue even after full en-Lightenment. I've seen videos of the great Indian sage Ramana Maharshi sitting in *samadhi*, and his head was spontaneously bobbing up and down from the force of the *Shakti* flowing through him. Adi Da had a great line regarding the invasive power of the *Shakti*: "When the Lord makes contact with you, he doesn't send down a grinning photograph; he takes you by the neck."

CHAPTER SIX

Holy Surrender (Perfect Poverty)

Surrender and Communion

It seems to me that thinking about spiritual life in terms of an electrical circuit is unnecessarily complicated. As I see it, spiritual life can reduced to a single principle: surrendering, or letting go.

You're right, and wrong. Yes, spiritual life can be reduced to a single principle, but that principle is *not* surrender, that principle is: *consciously abiding in the Spirit*—and you can only consciously abide in the Spirit when you integrate the disciplines of Divine Communion and surrender (or letting go).

If you seriously, *exclusively* practice surrendering, or letting go of your thoughts from moment to moment, you'll find that it is an arduous task that never ends (even if you've been baptized by the Holy Spirit). This is because self-emptying (or spiritual poverty) when practiced outside the context of Divine Communion is not an integral, or holistic, practice. This is not to say that randomly totally letting go outside the context of the practice of communion is not a beneficial practice—it is, and I highly recommend it; it is just to emphasize the fact that you cannot build a Spirit-full life on the *secondary* principle of poverty, or self-surrender. My suggestion to you is this: Spend several days devoting yourself exclusively to the practice of moment-to-moment letting go, and judge for yourself if self-emptying is the great "single principle" of spiritual life. My guess is that long before the several days are up, your "poverty" experiment will convince you that it isn't.

From what you're saying, it sounds like surrender not only isn't the primary principle of spiritual life, it's not even really a primary spiritual practice—and this contradicts your earlier designation of it as one.

You're correct, in a way. Although I designate surrender and Divine Communion as the two primary practices, surrender is really secondary to Divine Communion. Divine Communion has primacy over surrender, because without the conscious force engendered by Divine Communion, letting go has little spiritual significance. But once you plug into the Source, then letting go is equal in importance to Divine Communion, because if you don't let go, the Spirit-current can't flow. Ohm's Law provides us with a perfect analogy in this matter. If you plug a switched-on electrical device into a socket (source) and generate voltage (force), the amperage (current energy) of the circuit is directly proportional to the voltage and inversely proportional to the ohms (resistance). If we apply this to spirituality, then spiritual voltage (the conscious force engendered by Divine Communion) and spiritual ohms (the reduction of resistance effected by letting go) are equal in effect relative to increasing spiritual amperage (Spirit-current energy).

In practical terms, what are you saying?

That surrender should primarily be practiced in place—in the context of Divine Communion rather than as an exclusive discipline. Divine Communion (conscious connectedness) is the primary discipline, and letting go naturally follows after you plug into the Source, the Divine Presence. The cosmos is built on Consciousness, not on surrender, which is a derivative principle.

Once you lock in to the Spirit-current and can channel Grace, then Divine Communion and surrender essentially merge into the single, fundamental principle of *conscious resting in Light-energy*. This principle can still be referred to as Divine Communion (in its "en-Light-ened" form)—and when this en-Light-ened Communion becomes a disciple's constant state, then he has attained Divine Union, the acme of spiritual life.

The Three Sacred Vows and Communion

Is your emphasis on the primacy of communion over surrender unique? Or do various spiritual traditions concur with you?

It's hardly unique at all. For example, in Christianity, a monastic takes three sacred vows: *obedience*, *chastity*, and *poverty*. Obedience is a synonym for communion, chastity for living in the Spirit, and poverty for surrender. The obedient disciple *atones* for his sin (of disobedient separateness) from the Divine by practicing conscious *at-one-ment* with the virgin Spirit, the clear, or chaste, Light-energy from on high. In order to receive the inflow of Light-energy, he must "impoverish," or empty, himself. Like the Holy Chalice, he must be an empty cup, ready to be filled with Divine Elixir.

To the discerning, Ohm's Law is implicit in the Three Sacred Vows. And if Jesus returns, he will doubtless explicate the connection between electricity and the Sacred Vows. I personally have great affinity for the Vows, because they pithily and perfectly summarize what real spiritual life is all about.

Poverty and Nothingness

Poverty is self-emptiness, and in the method of Communion that you teach, you recommend that disciples initially focus their attention on the void, empty space. My question is: What is the ontological status of this emptiness or formlessness, this divine Nothingness that various schools of mysticism deify?

There is no such thing as an ineffable Nothingness underlying and transcending the Godhead, the Divine Being, which is Consciousness-Energy (or *Siva-Shakti*). The universe was not created *ex nihilo*, because something cannot come out of nothing. Prior to the Big Bang (Creation), the Energy of timeless and spaceless Consciousness existed as pure potential. When the Big Bang occurred (some 14 billion years ago, according to astrophysicists), time and space came into existence, as the "programmed" Energy emanated from the Divine Being-Consciousness crystallized into the universe, the cosmic order of matter, energy, and life.

Nothingness, non-existence, is a zero, and as such, it has no ontological status. Its value is purely as a derivative concept to indicate the absence of something. All things can be reduced to energy, but not to nothingness, and the fact that scientists cannot create a vacuum devoid of subatomic particles and energy proves this. Mystics sometimes refer to the Divine as the Vacuum-Plenum, because if an initiate empties his mind, he is flooded with spiritual energy. But this does not transform absence into the ontological equal and opposite of Presence. Presence is the *absolute* Context; emptiness is merely the *relative* lack of content. The more the initiate empties his mind, the more the Divine shines through him, as the dissolved mind-forms transmute into spiritual Energy. In other words, the Divine Being-Consciousness is Energy, not an ineffable Nothingness.

The great mystic Meister Eckhart summarizes poverty of the spirit as "wanting nothing, knowing nothing, and having nothing." In other words, the "Ohms pole" of spiritual practice is about self-emptying on every level of life. But self-emptying is not an end unto itself. It is simply the means to create an open receptacle, a Eucharistic chalice, for the Spirit to pour into and fill.

Self-emptying, psychical Ohms reduction, is an essential component of Eucharistic, or Electrical, spiritual life, but to equate God with emptiness or nothingness is a grievous spiritual error.

Emptiness and Meditation

But you recommend meditation on empty space.

Empty space is not "nothing." If space is nothing, then why do scientists tell us that the gravity of planetary bodies curves it? Moreover, gravity even exists in space, and physicists refer to this minute amount of gravity as "microgravity."

Although space is not "nothing," it is an excellent object of contemplation, a wonderful portal to the Holy Spirit. In fact, when I teach people how to meditate, I instruct them to "gaze into space" as a means to establishing themselves in Plugged-in Presence. The contemplative gaze into empty space is a fundamental practice in Tibetan Dzogchen, and it leads to empowered Holy Communion. The "void" is not void, and once you've been baptized by the Holy One, emptiness "dances" as bliss-*full* Light-energy.

Emptiness serves two functions in spiritual life: as an ideal object of meditation, and as the voiding of one's mind in order to provide inner "space" for the invasion of the Spirit. In other words, the void is a gateway to the Absolute, not the Absolute itself.

A New Earth

Will the meek inherit Earth, or was that just wishful thinking by Jesus?

I've often joked that the meek will inherit the earth only if scientists can bioengineer a docile cockroach (which could be the only living creature to survive a nuclear holocaust). Judging from the past two millennia and the current world situation, it doesn't appear likely that the "impoverished" will take over the reins of the planet any time soon. In fact, just the opposite appears to be the case, as the international banking cartel, the de facto New World Order boss, is firmly in control of Spaceship Earth. And with the U.S. "Federal" Reserve (an unaudited private corporation that specializes in counterfeiting) printing "greenbacks" (fiat currency) at a record rate, poverty is hardly in vogue at the present time.

Jesus isn't the only Avatar to preach poverty in the Spirit as the way to mankind's earthly salvation. Lao Tzu, the legendary Taoist sage, in the *Tao Te Ching*, says, "By his non-action the sage governs the world." But if we look at China now, more than twenty-five hundred years after Lao Tzu, we don't see surrendered sages governing the people; we see corrupt despots, evil state capitalists, ruling the land with an iron fist.

One could argue that Lao Tzu means the unattached sage "governs" the world by not being involved in its machinations, that even though he is in the world, he is not of it; and by virtue of his above-ness, he is the true master, or governor, of worldly reality. Likewise, one could claim that Jesus means almost the same: that the spiritually "impoverished" are really rich in Grace, and thus the inheritors of the only true or permanent wealth available on the planet.

In the *Christian Courier*, an online Christian journal, author Wayne Jackson argues that, biblically speaking, "meek" doesn't really mean meek. According to Jackson, "meek," in the Greek New Testament, is from the Greek term *praus*, which denotes "strength brought under control." Jackson informs us that the "ancient Greeks employed the term to describe a horse tamed to the bridle."

Spiritually speaking, the "strength" brought under control or "horse tamed" by an accomplished yogi, or completely impoverished disciple, is the wild and violent *Shakti*, the flaming Baptist Fire. Moreover, when the *Shakti* is tamed, so is the mind; therefore, "meek" disciples are really powerful Spirit-full ones possessing the integral mind-spirit combination to righteously "rule" or "inherit" the Earth. Consequently, after the New World Order gang significantly trashes the planet—but hopefully before it is able to execute its plan of implanting a computer chip into the brain of every human (go to Youtube.com and punch in Aaron Russo/ Nicholas Rockefeller/ RFID chip for video evidence)—the "sheeple," finally, truly "meek," will spiritually and politically awaken, and reclaim their just "inheritance," the Earth.

What you're saying about the New World Order is very interesting. Can you recommend any material on the subject?

Watch Stefan Molyneux's video *The Story of Your Enslavement* at Youtube.com; Google and read the essay *The Anatomy of the State*, by Murray Rothbard; get the books *The Creature from Jekyll Island: A Second Look at the Federal Reserve*, by G. Edward Griffin, and *The True Story of the Bilderberg Group*, by Daniel Estulin.

CHAPTER SEVEN

The Essence of the Sermon on the Mount

The Electrical Basis of Jesus' Message

Where in the Bible is the electrical nature of Christianity alluded to?

It is most clearly alluded to in the Sermon on the Mount (the Gospel of Matthew, chapters 5, 6, and 7). In the Sermon on the Mount, Jesus discloses the core tenets of Christian discipleship, and to the discerning, these tenets implicitly point to the electrical nature of his teachings.

In Matthew 6:22, Jesus says, "The light of the body is the eye: if therefore thine eye be single, thy whole body shall be full of light." Although this statement is baffling to the esoterically challenged, its meaning is clear to mystics: If one's eye (awareness) is single (one-pointedly focused on the Divine), then Divine Light-energy (the Holy Spirit) will infill one's body. In other words, en-Light-enment of the whole body naturally follows Divine (or Holy) Communion. From an electrical perspective, the conscious force that the disciple generates by plugging into the Divine Presence (or "Socket") is analogous to *voltage*, and the en-Light-ening Spirit-current that this single-eyed focusing pulls down is akin to *amperage*.

In Matthew 7:7, Jesus says "Ask and it will be given to you; seek and you will find; knock and it will be opened to you." This saying builds on 6:22 by applying single-pointed awareness to the practice of prayer. When the disciple practices being present to the Divine, *true prayer* (asking for God's Grace, His Blessing Power) serves to lock him into the Holy One and prepares him to receive His Spirit. Once sufficient spiritual voltage has been generated by the disciple's plugged-in presence, all he has to do is to reduce *ohms* (resistance) by letting go and opening to the inflowing Light-energy from on high. Jesus alludes to this effortlessness in Matthew 6:28, when he says, "Consider the lilies of the field, how they grow: yet they neither toil nor spin." This "poverty of the spirit," when practiced in the context of empowered Holy Communion, leads the baptized disciple to eternal rest in God. And Jesus makes this clear in Matthew 5:3, when he says, "Blessed be the poor in spirit, for theirs is the kingdom of heaven."

The essential message of the Sermon on the Mount is: Connect to God via one-pointed presence and/or prayer, and then allow His Will (or Power and Glory) to en-Light-en (or save) you. In Matthew 6:5 to 6:13, Jesus describes the Model Prayer, and the essence of this prayer is to call upon God and allow Him, via His Power (the Holy Spirit), to deliver you from sin and suffering into the heavenly kingdom.

Follow Your Own Spiritual Compass

How about judgment? Does that also have to be relinquished by the disciple?

Prior to your eye (or awareness) being single (or clear and unobstructed), judgment is typically an impediment to the spiritual process. But once you are established in pure presence, then judgment no longer binds you. Jesus makes this clear in Matthew 7:5: "Thou hypocrite, first cast out the beam of thine own eye; and then shalt thou see clearly to cast out the mote of thy brother's eye." But Jesus doesn't even rule out judgment for those with an occluded eye—as long as they don't mind being judged (and exposed) in return. In Matthew 7:1, he says, "Judge not, that ye be not judged." In other words, it's okay to dish out shit, if you don't mind having it thrown back at you.

The key point regarding your question about judgment is this: What Jesus or any guru says should be considered in the light of your own experience. Begin to live real spiritual life yourself, and see if judgment obstructs your practice. If it does, strive to relinquish it. If it doesn't, continue to sagaciously exercise it. Real spiritual life should translate into the awakening of real intelligence, and this intelligence, which stems from your own experience of the Spirit, will tell you what helps and what hinders your discipleship.

Wow! What you're saying sounds like it borders on apostasy.

Hardly. In fact, I consider myself a dyed-in-the-wool apostle of the *Truth*. But dogmatically following Jesus or Buddha or anyone else is not the same as religiously adhering to Truth. The Truth will set you free, not Jesus or Buddha. Jesus and Buddha were avataric masters who realized Truth and originated great teachings (or en-Light-enment maps) for their disciples. But the map is not the "Territory," so if you find Jesus' "directions" in some way counter to your own experience, then by all means feel free to follow your own "spiritual compass." Just be sure that your compass points in the direction of Truth and not in the direction of your subjective whims.

What do you mean by "Truth"?

Truth is the recognition of Reality. Genuine spiritual life is simply, and only, a life devoted to Truth, a life devoted to recognizing, and abiding in, the Real—Consciousness-Power (the Father-Holy Spirit). When you perfectly abide in the Father-Holy Spirit, then you spontaneously abide *as* a Christ (the True Self). Jesus was the man, and the *Christ* is the Consciousness that he realized.

Build your Spiritual Life on the Rock

In the Sermon on the Mount, Jesus says that those who hear and do his sayings are building their spiritual life on the rock. It sounds like that "rock" is essentially the Eucharist.

Very true. The Eucharist is indeed the mystical message implicit in his sermon. And even his moral injunctions have a mystical, or yogic, basis, in that observance of them can serve to free one's attention and energy for the practice of Divine Communion. In other words, if you turn the other cheek, love your enemies, do charitable deeds in secret, and so forth, your moral purity can serve to intensify your connection to the Divine. But in reality, many saintly people who do Jesus' sayings do not awaken to the Holy Spirit, while innumerable "sinners" do. For example, in India, "left-handed" tantric practitioners often flout conventional religious morality and intentionally engage in lewd, socially unacceptable behavior in order to awaken or intensify the flow of *Shakti*, the Spirit-current. Thus, the real rock of spiritual life is simply Spirit Communion itself, exclusive of the normative behavior prescribed by Jesus or anyone else.

So traditional Christian morality can be dispensed with on the mystical path?

True, or rational, morality, such as non-killing, non-stealing, and non-lying, clearly should *not* be dispensed with. But some Biblical moral injunctions, particularly those in the Old Testament, are antiquated and cockamamie: for example, stoning people to death for working on the Sabbath. The Bible is by no means the last word on ethics, and I suggest that students of normative philosophy compare Christian morality with Buddhist ethics and Ayn Rand's Objectivist ethics. You can Google these terms and find plenty of information available on the Web.

CHAPTER EIGHT

Prayer and Meditation (Aligning Yourself with the Divine)

Light on the Practice of Plugged-in Presence

What is the difference between prayer and meditation?

If prayer is practiced properly, then it is the same as meditation. In other words, if it is practiced intently and one-pointedly, with full focus or concentration, then it becomes a meditative (or yogic) spiritual exercise rather than a random, haphazard petitioning of the Divine. True prayer does not involve begging God for favors; it simply means *meditatively (or intently, one-pointedly, and sometimes incessantly)* asking God to bless you with His Grace, His Spirit-power. God's Blessing Power is the same as His Will (which is to en-Light-en you). Therefore the Model Prayer, in essence, is simply to say: "Thy Will be done," and then to allow the supernal Light-energy to irradiate your whole bodily-being. Until your prayer bears Fruit (Grace), you must continue to beseech God to bless you. When His Spirit-power descends into and through you, you can relax your efforts and simply channel the Divine Blessing.

Real meditation, like true prayer, is all about "positioning" yourself to receive Grace. It is simply the practice of (directly and immediately) aligning your whole person with the Divine, so you can commune with and channel the Higher Power. In a word, it is *Relationship*—whole-bodily oneness with the Holy One. When, in your practice of real meditation, you become aware that you have retracted from at-one-ment with the Divine (and into mental reverie and/or disturbing emotions), simply reassume, or attempt to reassume, the *asana* (or psycho-physical "position") of *relationship*.

Do you have any specific instructions for establishing this Divine connection?

Yes, and they all pertain to *consciously* "positioning" yourself to receive the Benediction. You should experiment with my recommendations and use the ones that best enable you to plug into the Divine Presence and pull down Divine Power. I have presented these instructions in our previous discussions, but they bear repeating—and each time I present them I do so in a somewhat different way, which may provide you with some new insights into the practice of Divine Communion. Although I will number the recommendations, be advised that they overlap and intertwine and do not have to be practiced in the order in which I present them.

> 1) Sit upright on a chair (Note: slightly tucking your chin will naturally straighten your spine.) Rest your hands (palms down) on your thighs. Experiment with sitting on the edge of the chair (or a bench) versus with your back against its back. Alternatively, you can sit cross-legged on the floor (preferably with a meditation cushion, such as a Zen zafu, underneath your buttocks).

> 2) Establish what the Buddha called "self-possession." In other words, feel yourself as the whole body, and then be consciously present as the whole body, the whole psycho-physical being. Randomly focusing your attention

on your third-eye area and hands will help enable you to coincide with your body, and thereby heal the body-mind split. When you consciously inhabit your whole body and are wholly, or integrally, present to the whole (the totality of existence), you are in proper position to receive and conduct the Force-flow from above.

3) "Gaze" into empty space. If you are "self-possessed," this "gaze" will amount to being whole-bodily present to (or in direct relationship to) the void. As soon as you become aware that you have retracted from your "position" of conscious connectedness to (or single-pointed focus on) the void, simply reassume, or attempt to reassume, your "stance" of holistic at-one-ment. To this end, you can randomly use an enquiry (such as "Avoiding relationship?") to instigate your resumption of communion with the void. When the void begins to "shine," it is experienced as Divine Presence; and when the Power of the Presence pours down upon you, then "emptiness" has morphed into Spirit, and your "gaze into space" has transmuted into empowered Holy Communion.

4) Randomly focus your attention on your breath (by being in direct relationship to your breathing cycle). When the breath "comes alive" as prana-shakti, palpable intensified life-energy, simply remain present to it. Your communion with the breath cycle will transmute into true, or infused, Holy Communion when the prana-shakti morphs into the Holy Spirit, the great Shakti poured down from above.

5) Totally relax your body (including your head) and utterly let go of your mind. (Once you are able to

connect to the Shakti, you will directly experience that letting go intensifies the force-flow (or pressure) of the Spirit-current. Be an empty cup, ready to be filled with Holy Water from above. When you experience the Benediction, the Divine downpour, remain motivelessly present to it. Your searchless beholding of the Shakti will enable you to spontaneously merge with it.

These technical meditation (and prayer) instructions are all about facilitating communion, and then union, with the Divine. It is up to you to test them out and determine how useful they are for your Christian yoga practice. Truly speaking, no spiritual practice, in and of itself, is holy or sacred. The only "Thing" holy or sacred is the Holy One Himself (including His Holy Spirit). Therefore, whatever practices bring you into communion with the Holy One are the ones you should employ.

The practice of real (or divine) meditation is identical to the practice of real (or divine) Christianity, which is identical to the practice of real (or divine) yoga. Real (or divine) yoga is simply, *and only*, the practice of uniting one's individual soul (or consciousness) with universal Spirit (or Light-energy). When the two vines of the Absolute (or Divine Being)—consciousness and Spirit—are permanently united in a yogi, then he awakens as en-Light-ened Consciousness (or conscious Light). The awakened yogi (now a Christ or Buddha) inheres in the Absolute, and his Spirit-full Soul is eternally one with the Divine Being (or "Father"). And this immutable "State" (really a non-state) of Divine Union is called Enlightenment (or Self-realization) by Hindu yogis, Nirvana (or Buddhahood) by Buddhists, and Heaven (or Christ-Consciousness) by Christian mystics.

Two Great Mystics and the Practice of Plugged-in Presence

What gurus have taught a spiritual method similar to Plugged-in Presence?

Too many to mention all the names. What I've attempted to do with my Electrical Spiritual Paradigm is to both essentialize and creatively "repackage," the Dharma (Truth Teaching) of the great mystics who, implicitly or explicitly, taught Eucharistic spirituality, the Plugged-in Presence method. In the twentieth century, J. Krishnamurti and Adi Da, most notably, taught Dharmas akin to mine, and I am indebted to them for their Wisdom teachings. But I want to mention two great fourteenth-century mystics who, perhaps more than coincidentally, taught my "brand" of mysticism.

I'll start with Meister Eckhart. In his wonderful text *The Mystical Thought of Meister Eckhart*, author Bernard McGinn identifies three spiritual processes that represent the core of Eckhart's sermons: *breaking through*, *detaching*, and *birthing*. Breaking through is analogous to *plugging in* (and thereby penetrating to the Other Side), detaching is akin to *poverty* (letting go), and birthing is the process of becoming Christ-like via the *power* of Now (the Holy Spirit). The Electrical Spiritual Paradigm is implicit in Eckhart's teachings, and if he were alive and preaching today, he would doubtless make the connection between his three core processes and Ohm's Law.

When, several years ago, I first read *The Precious Treasury of the Way of Abiding*, by Longchen Rabjam, one of the greatest Tibetan Dzogchen masters, I was so excited I nearly fell off my chair. Rabjam's book was a discourse on the four cardinal themes of Dzogchen—*spontaneous presence*, *oneness*, *openness*, and *ineffability*— that virtually mirrored my still nascent Electrical Spiritual

Paradigm. Spontaneous (or direct and immediate) presence plus oneness equaled *plugged-in presence* (or voltage); openness equated with *poverty* (or ohms reduction); and ineffability referred to the unspeakable, indefinable nature of all phenomena, including the "dynamic energy" (Rabjam's term), or *power* (or amperage), that naturally accompanies awakened awareness or presence. Moreover, in the other Rabjam text I was simultaneously reading, *A Treasure Trove of Spiritual Transmission*, he described the *togal* practice of relaxing in the *continuum of radiance*, which is akin to resting in the Spirit and receiving, or channeling, its Light-energy. *Togal* is one of the two fundamental meditation practices in Dzogchen; the other is *trekcho*, the practice of cutting or breaking through one's resistance to get to the continuum of radiance (the Other Side). These two practices are also the foundational ones of Eucharistic, or Electrical, spirituality. In other words, Rabjam's Dzogchen = Eckhart's Christian mysticism ⁻ the Plugged-in Presence method (which in its "awakened" form includes channeling Grace, the continuum of Divine radiance).

True Prayer

Can you describe what you call True Prayer in more detail?

True prayer is simply asking God to bless you, and then receiving His Blessing Power, the Holy Spirit. But in order to make yourself a fit receptacle for the Benediction, the Descent of Divine Grace, you first need to "self-possess" (or integrally "organize") yourself. In other words, as I have just described in my recommendations, you need to consciously inhabit your body, feel yourself as the whole body, and then be present as the whole body. Once you have "self-possessed" yourself (which can be done in a "feeling" flash) and "positioned" yourself (in direct, immediate relationship to the open space in front of you), all you have to "do" is to remain present (and plugged-in), silently ask

God to bless you, and wait to receive the Gift from on high. Once the Holy Spirit invades your being, you can either searchlessly behold Its Splendor and Glory, intensely merge with It, or utterly empty yourself, which will serve to magnify the Heavenly Downpour.

How should we phrase the mystical prayer?

However you want. I just periodically, silently say, "Bless me." God doesn't need a speech from you; he just needs to know what you want. But if you're not properly, or "prayerfully," positioned, you won't be a fit receptacle for the Benediction. To properly position myself, I periodically enquire in the form: "Avoiding relationship?" This enables me to maintain, and also serves to intensify, my Divine connection. It could be said that the "Bless Me" prayer and the "Relationship" enquiry constitute a yin and a yang, with the prayer serving as a "receptive" portal to the Divine, and the enquiry as a "connective" one.

Repetitive Prayer and Mantra Meditation

I am unable to get to the level of infused contemplation. *What type of* acquired contemplation *do you recommend?*

Anyone who finds himself incapable of developing an empowered practice of Holy Communion should experiment with repetitive prayer and/or mantra meditation. I recommend two books relative to this subject: *The Way of a Pilgrim and the Pilgrim Continues His Way,* and *The Essential Swami Ramdas. The Way of a Pilgrim and the Pilgrim Continues His Way* is about a nineteenth-century peasant who devotes himself to the practice of ceaseless prayer via repetition of the Jesus Prayer ("Lord Jesus Christ, son of God, have mercy on me, a sinner"). *The Essential Swami Ramdas* is an anthology of the writings of Swami Ramdas, a great twentieth-century Hindu *bhakti* (or devotional) yogi who attained Self-realization by ceaselessly repeating the mantra *Om Sri Ram, Jai Ram, Jai Jai Ram* (which means, "God who is at once Truth and Power, victory to Thee, victory, victory to Thee").

Anyone who decides to practice repetitive prayer or mantra meditation (*japa*) should experiment with prayer beads as an adjunct. Prayer beads involve conscious use of the hands, which helps integrate the body into the practice. (If you Google prayer beads, you'll find a wide variety of beads available.)

There are two keys to successful practice of repetitive prayer and *japa*: one-pointed focus on repetition of the phrase or mantra, and a devotional mindset. If you are a true devotee of the Lord, you'll find that your love of God will translate into a natural focus on repetition of the sacred phrase or mantra.

A final point regarding ceaseless prayer or *japa*: It's not really "ceaseless." In other words, when the practice leads you into the Spirit or just becomes oppressive, that is a signal to surrender, to totally let go and let be. Constant repetitive prayer or *japa* is an intense spiritual practice, and it is important to periodically relax and let go to in order to release bodily tension and allow the Spirit a chance to move into and through you.

Can we practice both mantra meditation and real (or divine) meditation?

Of course you can. Again, I repeat my "mantra": Whatever awakens you to the Spirit is what you should practice. Repetitive prayer and *japa* lead to contact with Spirit, and once that contact occurs, you have made the leap from *acquired contemplation* to *infused contemplation* and are then able to practice empowered Holy Communion.

Vanishing the Mind

I am constantly troubled by disturbing thoughts. What do you recommend to stop them?

Holy Communion. Once you awaken to, and receive, the Holy Spirit, you'll find that its influx of Light-energy will outshine your mind, literally vanishing thoughts. The problem, of course, is that you can't remain in that state of Grace, and as soon as you lose your Divine connection, you again suffer from disturbing mind-forms, which can seem worse than before because now you are now more sensitive to them. The radical (or gone-to-the-root) spiritual solution is simply to reconnect to the Spirit and allow its Power to "heal" you by irradiating your discordant mind-forms. Spirit Power is a Blessing (and Blissing) Energy, and superfluous thoughts and unsettling emotions are naturally obviated in, and by, its radiant Intensity.

Short of Holy Communion—the face-to-Face encounter with the Divine and reception of Its mind-incinerating Intensity (or Saving Grace)—a disciple must resort to less-than-Holistic (or Holy) approaches to ridding himself of unwanted mind-forms. These approaches include repetitive prayer, *japa*, and basic forms of meditation (aimed at focusing the mind on a particular object—outer and physical, or inner and subtle). But for a more advanced yogi, there are more direct ways to vanish the mind. He can dispassionately watch it, which tends to dissolve it, because one cannot be both the watcher and the thinker at the same time; he can willfully disidentify from thoughts, rejecting them as they arise; or, if he is a tantric yogi, he can neither accept nor reject arising thoughts, which allows them to "self-liberate," or spontaneously dissolve. Although these "gnostic" approaches to silencing the mind can be very effective, they demand a conscious effort by the yogi; but since all efforts are spasmodic, so are the results. The truth is, the only way to be free of the mind for sustained periods of time is to be able to rest in the Grace (or Spirit)-current—and the only way to do that is via the practice of empowered Holy Communion.

But the mind always reappears once it's vanished. So permanently getting rid of the mind cannot amount to enlightenment.

Exactly. The point of real spirituality isn't to permanently get rid of the mind; it's to awaken to the Spirit. Temporary emptying of the mind is an essential component of spiritual life, but once you are established in the Spirit, you can rest in the Light-energy continuum, and allow the radiant Downpour to outshine your mind, rendering your discordant thoughts impotent. When you are permanently, effortlessly able to abide in this Grace from on high, then you are no longer subject to rebirth; you have attained Nirvana, and will dwell forever more in Heaven, the Divine Domain.

Aids to Prayer and Meditation

Apart from the core practices of acquired and infused contemplation, are there any other disciplines that you can recommend?

Yes, ones that deal with *chi* (or *prana*). Tai chi and chi gung are excellent ancillary practices, and the practice of touch-for-health healing modalities that involve channeling energy, such as Jin Shin Jyutsu and Reiki, will also help you spiritually.

Are there any particulars relative to right living that you feel are especially important?

Yes, diet and sex, especially for beginners. Regarding diet, it is preferable to eat small, easily digestible meals of natural, unprocessed food. Anyone who has a sensitive digestive system should read *Food Combining Made Easy*, by Herbert Shelton. I personally have a temperamental stomach, and by avoiding difficult combinations—such as acid (tomatoes and citrus) with starch, and sugar (including fruit and dried fruit) with starch—I have significantly reduced my digestive problems. Cutting out or down on stimulating spices, such as garlic, onions, and pepper, will also help quiet both the passions and the mind. Caffeine should also be discontinued or curtailed, since it makes the mind hyper and harder to control. Alcohol should be avoided, because it dulls the mind; and pot is far worse than booze because it fogs the brain for up to a month after it's smoked. Regarding sex, the less you indulge, the better off spiritually you will be. And masturbation should be discontinued. It might not give you pimples or stunt your growth, as old-time Christian moralists used to claim, but it will drain your subtle life-force and negatively—psychically as well as energetically—impact your spiritual life.

That sounds like quite a commitment. I doubt if I'm ready for it.

No "commitment" is necessary. And God isn't going to punish you if you're a "bad boy" and, say, get drunk and jerk off. All that will happen is that your spiritual life will temporarily suffer because you won't have the free attention and subtle life-energy to deeply commune with God. Thus, rather than God punishing you, you will be punishing yourself. Moreover, you don't have to adopt all the recommended disciplines, and you don't have to adopt the ones you do all at once. What you may find is that once you get a hit of God Intoxication, you'll want to do whatever you can to maximize your capacity to connect to the Divine, and if that means a strict lifestyle, so be it. But even if you decide to be an unrepentant hedonist, that is no excuse for not continuing to practice Plugged-in Presence. In other words, it's not that you must purify yourself via the salutary disciplines, and then you can begin to practice communion. No, the way it works is that you begin the spiritual practice, and then in conjunction with it, you simultaneously, to one degree or another, work on purifying your bodymind, making it a fit "temple" for receiving and conducting the Spirit. The word *contemplate* means to receive the Spirit via the bodily *temple*; therefore, my advice to you is to make your psycho-physical temple a clean and empty "space" that attracts, or draws down, the Deity.

After a disciple develops a strong, consistent spiritual practice, he may find that the disciplines hardly matter, that virtually nothing obstructs his communion practice. For example, I chug down a couple of double espressos daily and periodically sample fine scotch, but my practice is unaffected. Real spiritual life isn't about becoming a dry puritan; it's *only* about living in the Spirit. And the extent to which salutary disciplines help you commune with God is the extent to which they need to be practiced.

When you talked about diet, you didn't mention vegetarianism. Do you recommend a vegetarian diet? And if so, do you recommend a vegan diet?

No, I don't recommend vegetarianism, and I'm particularly opposed to a vegan diet. A typical vegetarian diet (even one with plenty of grains) is too alkaline—greatly exceeding the optimal 2/1 alkaline/acid ratio that the renowned Price-Pottenger Nutrition Foundation recommends. I speak from personal experience regarding the dangers of alkalosis. In the early 1970s, I was a vegetarian for a few years, and I permanently messed up my body by living on a "naked ape" vegan diet of mainly raw fruits, vegetables, nuts, and seeds. Although some people (due to their blood type and body chemistry) can thrive on a vegetarian diet, most do better as omnivores. An in-depth consideration of diet is outside the scope of this spiritual discussion, but I do want to say that I'm somewhat of an expert on nutrition, and hope to someday write a book exposing the dangers of vegetarianism.

If you don't believe in vegetarian diet, what kind of diet do you recommend?

The diet that I generally recommend is the Paleo diet, which is detailed in the book *The Paleo Diet*, by Loren Cordain. I can certainly understand why someone would be a vegetarian for moral reasons, but my suggestion to anyone interested in finding the optimal diet is this: Try the Paleo diet for few weeks and see how you feel and function on it versus on vegetarian fare. Also notice if eating flesh foods negatively impacts your spiritual practice. If it does, try cutting out red meat and sticking to fish and poultry. Another book that I highly recommend is *Ayurveda: The Science of Self-Healing*, by Vasant Lad. Ayurveda is an Indian system of health and healing that enables one to determine his elemental constitution, and therefore the foods, herbs, and activities that are best for him. A consultation with an Ayurvedic practitioner who can read pulses will provide you with unique insights into your body.

The Homegrown Temple

Is it a good idea to create a special, holy meditation space? Or is that just a form of spiritual materialism?

Most disciples find that a personal sacred meditation space or room elevates their spiritual practice. Such a "divine milieu" not only serves to quiet the mind and open one to the Holy One, but also can become a veritable hotbed for the *Shakti*. Mother *Shakti*, the Blessed Virgin Spirit, is drawn to holy environs, and by "building" your own mini-temple and reverently serving it with worshipful care, prayer, and meditation, you, in effect, create a *bodhimandala*, an "en-Light-enment circle," or sanctum, that functions to attract, or pull down, Divine Power.

Swami Sivananda, the late, great Indian guru, exhorted his devotees to dedicate a room exclusively to meditation. He insisted that the room should be kept under lock and key, so as to prevent it from being polluted by gross, worldly vibrations. It is up to you if you want to follow the Swami's advice or just establish a sacred space in the midst of your regular living environment.

Cycles of *Sadhana*

Sometimes my meditation sessions are great—lots of bliss, and my mind is naturally quiet. And other times they are horrible—lots of disturbing emotions, and my mind is crazy.

That's spiritual life, a veritable roller coaster. And the ups and downs can occur within a very short time frame. That's why I recommend several shorter meditation sessions a day rather than, say, two long ones. For instance, if your first meditation session on a particular morning is going poorly, cut it short and try again a little later. Often times, the difference between two separate, consecutive sessions can be like night and day. And those times when you're Blessed with/by intense, downpouring *Shakti*, you should extend your sessions.

Do lunar cycles affect meditation?

Absolutely. And full moons are a particularly auspicious time for spiritual practice (or *sadhana*). The *Shakti* flows freely when the moon is full, so it is a good idea to ratchet up your *sadhana* on those days. When a full moon occurs, the sun and moon are 180 degrees opposite from each other, which results in maximum cosmic polarization relative to the earth plane, and thus maximum potential spiritual "electricity," or *Shakti*, for those who have been baptized.

What can you say about the gunas?

The Hindu yoga traditions describe life as the "play of the *gunas*." The interplay, or cycling, of the *gunas*, the three essential "qualities," or energy modes, of existence—*Sattva* (balanced and clear), *Rajas* (active and restless), and *Tamas* (inert and dull)—results in a constantly changing psycho-physical "environment" for living organisms. For example, when *Sattva guna* predominates in a disciple, he should take advantage of the clear energy state and devote himself to meditation; when *Rajas guna* prevails, he should focus on constructive activity; and when *Tamas* overtakes him, he should rest and recharge his batteries.

The Self-realized being is above the *gunas*, the cyclic play of nature and its energies. Although his body is affected by the *gunas*, his consciousness isn't, as he is permanently rested in the Absolute, beyond conditional flux. But until one is en-Light-ened, it is a good idea to pay attention to the *gunas*, and act accordingly.

CHAPTER NINE

"See Me, Feel Me, Touch Me, Heal Me"

Deaf, Dumb, and Blind

I'm a Christian, and I find your teachings interesting. But where does Jesus fit into them? It seems like you're presenting the possibility of salvation without Jesus, and that is... well, heretical.

In the rock album *Tommy*, by the Who, Tommy, the pinball wizard, is deaf, dumb, and blind, which means he can't be told about Jesus, can't accept him as his savior, and can't be saved. But Tommy finds Salvation anyway, because Salvation has nothing to do with Jesus, who was simply a messenger (albeit an Avataric one) of the "Good News."

But Jesus said that the Way was through Him.

When Jesus *Christ* said, "The Way to the Father is through Me," he meant that Salvation is only possible through the *Christ*—the Self (or Buddha)-nature. The Christ (the Son, Soul, or Self) can be realized by any man who renounces his root-ego (his moment-to-moment psychical retraction from the Divine) and allows the Holy Spirit to en-Light-en (or divinize) him. Therefore, the Way (to Heaven, the Divine Domain) is not through Jesus, the *mortal* man, it is through the Christ, the *immortal* Soul (or Son), which, upon union with the Holy Spirit, realizes its (or his) oneness with God (the Father).

◇ ◇ ◇

But I have a personal relationship with Jesus…

No, you don't. You have a personal "relationship" with a concept or mental image of him. Since you were a child, you've seen pictures of a tall, lean, saintly-looking man with a beard. You formed mental images from the pictures, combined them with belief systems laid on you by the mainstream church, and— presto!—you've got a "relationship" with Jesus. But in reality, your "personal relationship" with Jesus is no different than the one a guy with his pants down and hand busy has with his favorite Internet porn star. In other words, it's *imaginary*.

This isn't to say that pictures of or thoughts about Jesus, or Buddha, or any dead saint, can't lead you into deep, *formless* communion; they can. It's simply to say that such images do not constitute a real relationship and should be recognized for what they are: *forms* that can potentially lead you into the Divine abyss, the great void, where the Spirit shines and engulfs you.

Whenever zealous mainstream Christians have tried to convert me by inviting me to have a "personal relationship" with Jesus, my reply has always been: "I'd love to have a personal relationship with Jesus, and as soon as you can introduce him to me, I'll worship him and accept him as my Guru and Savior." But so far, no one has been able to produce Jesus, and until someone does, I'll be like Tommy, and receive my spiritual sustenance by "touching," "feeling," and "seeing" God directly, sans a Divine-human intermediary.

"Sensing" God

What do you mean by "touching, feeling, and seeing God directly"?

"*Touching* God" means to directly contact, or commune with, the Spirit, God's living Energy. Once you've been baptized, *initiated* by the Holy One, you can, at times, freely plug into the Spirit and *feel* its presence (as radiant stillness), pressure (as an invasive, expansive force, particularly in the head region), and power (as a polarized "pulling" down the frontal line of the body). When you gaze upon, or consciously behold, God's radiant Splendor, that is called "*seeing* the Light."

To the radical nondual mystics, the forms of "sensing" (really, "supersensing") God that I have just described do *not* represent true experiences of God himself. Rather, they represent experiences of God's *theophany*, His *objective* manifestation as radiant Energy. God's radiance experienced over against oneself is always a dualistic experience, and as the radical nondual mystics correctly point out, God cannot be "known" (or "sensed," or "seen" and "felt") as an Object outside, or independent, of one's being. God can only be "known" or "sensed" "Subjectively," as Divine Beingness that is coincident with, yet transcendent over, one's individual being.

To the radical nondual mystics, "seeing God" occurs when the pulled-down Power, the descending Spirit-current, reaches the Sacred (or Mystic) Heart-center, just to the right of the center of one's chest. In that "space," the Holy Spirit (the "Bride") unites with the Son (the "Bridegroom"), and the yogi spontaneously realizes that his now free Soul (the yoked Bridegroom, or awakened Christ Consciousness) is forever inseparable from and coincident with the Divine Being. This radical nondual realization is sometimes called "seeing God," even though there is no Divine "Thing" or Being to be seen. Rather, the illumined yogi simply inheres as the transcendental *Seer*, or Self, the Christ-Consciousness that is coessential with God, the Divine Being-Consciousness.

When the illumined yogi inheres as the Seer, he not only "sees" (or "knows") himself as coincident with the Divine Being, he also "feels" (or bliss-fully enjoys) himself *as* That. In Hindu yoga, this spontaneous, nondual (or purely Subjective) enjoyment of one's Beingness is called the "Feeling of Being." Prior to Self-realization, the cutting of the Sacred Heart-knot, the yogi mainly experiences the *Shakti*, the Bliss-current, objectively, apart from, or over against, his individual being; but upon full en-Light-enment—the union of immanent *Siva* (the embodied Soul, or Christ) and transcendent *Shakti* (the divine Spirit, or Virgin Mother)—he eternally rests in heavenly Beatitude, forever enjoying unalloyed Bliss, the perfect and permanent feeling of nondual Beingness.

The "feeling of Being" sounds fantastic, but isn't it dependent on the senses and nervous system?

"Feeling" is not one of the five senses; it is the affective "function" of the soul (one's consciousness). "Seeing"—awareness or understanding—is the soul's other non-sensorial function. Although the soul functions temporally and spatially through the senses, it exists outside of time and space, and as such, was never born, and never dies. The soul (consciousness) is sometimes referred to by mystics as the "sixth sense," because the five senses are always dependent on it. In reality, it is consciousness, the soul, that sees, hears, smells, touches, and tastes; the senses are just "sub-functions," or nervous system extensions, of it. The feeling of Being is intrinsic to Being, so when a yogi awakens as Being-Consciousness, the Self, he also, naturally and spontaneously, feels his Beingness—and that feeling is inherently, and permanently, blissful because en-Light-enment, by definition, is the everlasting union of universal Spirit (the Bliss-current) with the individual soul.

The un-en-Light-ened person (or soul) experiences one limited (or contracted) feeling (or emotional reaction) after another in response to life, whereas the en-Light-ened being always enjoys the illimitable (or uncontracted) feeling of Being. And in Christian mysticism, this blissful, nondual feeling of Being is termed *Beatitude*.

In practical terms, how does one get to this blissful feeling of Being?

As the great mystic J. Krishnamurti says, "To be [unqualifiedly] related is to *be*." Therefore, when you are in unobstructed relationship, or communion, with the Holy Spirit, the Blessing/Blissing Power from above, then your blessed relationship will naturally morph into the blissful, nondual feeling of Being. But until one's Heart-knot is cut by Mother Shakti, the Holy Spirit, permanent abidance in Beatitude is not possible.

From a technical standpoint, the way to Beatitude is simple: Be directly and immediately whole-bodily present to the empty space in front of you. This direct awareness + oneness relative to the void is called the "gaze into space." At some point, the emptiness will begin to "dance," or "move," as *Shakti*, and your "gaze into space" will transmute into a "gaze upon the dynamic Splendor." When that occurs, just maintain your Holy connection and allow the radiant Energy, the Bliss-current, to penetrate you. At some point, the "boundary" between your consciousness (or soul) and the Light-energy (or Spirit) will dissolve, and as your *dualistic* contemplation of Spirit transmutes into *nondual* beingness, your feeling of blissful relatedness will simultaneously morph into the nondual feeling of Being.

The feeling of Being is tantamount to feeling *Divine*—because the yogi, at least temporarily, has united the two *vines* of the *Absolute* (Soul and Spirit). And in so doing, he has, at least temporarily, obtained *absolution*, redemption from the primal and primordial sin of egoic separation from the Divine Being.

Blind Faith

Where does faith come into the picture you've painted? The Bible teaches that faith is vital if one is to be saved.

Without conviction based on direct personal experience, faith is blind. Real faith follows, rather than precedes, contact with the Holy Spirit. Only someone who has been baptized by the Holy One can exercise true religious faith. Millions of people throughout history have been slaughtered simply because they refused to accept a religion or religious "savior" on faith alone. Conversion by the sword is the product of faith-based fanaticism, and a way to help end the violence is to universally encourage a mindset that emphasizes communion with the Spirit rather than exclusive belief in a particular religion.

CHAPTER TEN

The Essence of Christian Mysticism

A Brief Summary of the Heavenly Way

Can you summarize the way of a Christian mystic?

An esoteric Christian mystic seeks to duplicate Jesus' realization that "I and the Father are one." To this end, he practices the discipline that Jesus taught: the Holy Eucharist, communion with the Holy One via His Spirit. Once the infinite (or spaceless) Spirit unites with the mystic's soul, he achieves Divine Union and awakens as a Christ, a divinized (or en-Lightened) being eternally (or timelessly) one with the Father.

The Christian mystic takes three sacred vows: *obedience*, *chastity*, and *poverty*. Obedience is a synonym for Holy Communion. True, or radical, *obedience* means that as soon as the mystic notices he has lost his connection to the Holy Spirit, he reestablishes, or attempts to reestablish it. True, or radical, *chastity* means a life devoted to living in (or under) the pure, or *virgin*, Light-energy, the Holy Spirit. It means renouncing carnality and instead "embracing the bosom" of the Bliss-bestowing Virgin Mother. True, or radical, *poverty* means utterly emptying oneself of mind and desire in order to become an empty vessel, a holy chalice that can receive and contain the Benediction, the downpoured Spirit.

Traditional Christian mysticism identifies three stages in the divinization process: *purification*, *illumination*, and *union*. These stages overlap and intertwine and thus do not constitute a strict hierarchy. *Purification*, or purgation, is the painful psycho-physical *cleansing* that that the disciple undergoes in the divinization process. The invasion of radiant Light-energy into a sensitive human container is an intense ordeal; hence it is sometimes described as one of "blood, sweat, and tears." *Illumination*, the literal en-Light-enment of his whole person, or bodily being, is what the disciple experiences as he becomes progressively able to channel greater "measures" of Grace, the Blessing Power, or Gift, from above. As the illumination stage progresses, the disciple finds himself enjoying more and more experiences of *ecstatic* communion with the Deity. The term "ecstasy" means to stand outside oneself, and the free-standing devotee of the Divine simply rests in the Bliss-current from on high, the Supernal Influx, and allows God's eternal-life-giving "Blood" to be poured upon him. When the Holy Blood, the Ambrosial Flow from above, pours into the disciple's Sacred Heart-center, he experiences Divine Union, as his soul merges with the Grace-full Nectar. And when the in-pouring Blood severs his Heart-knot, the Divine Union becomes permanent; and the deified disciple dwells forever more in the Divine Domain, Heaven.

Some mystics have recognized additional phases or stages in the divinization process. Although most of these seem superfluous to me, I do agree that *identity* should be recognized as a fourth stage, spontaneously following *union*. In reality, *identity* does not represent a higher stage than union; it is simply the spontaneous realization of one's identity as the Self (or Christ) that naturally accompanies it. *Identity* was not included as a fourth stage in Christian mysticism for fear of the Orthodox Church. Because Christian mysticism arose and developed in the context of the

Orthodox Church, it was verboten for any Christian yogi to proclaim himself a Self-realized being, consubstantial with the Father. That status was reserved for Jesus, and any mystic who even alluded to his own Christ-like nature risked serious consequences.

The Spiritual Journey of a Christian Hermeticist

Is the way of a Christian mystic any different than that of a Christian Hermeticist?

Only in that the Hermeticist marries occult or cabalistic knowledge with Christianity and employs some different terms to describe the mystical process. The Western esoteric tradition derives heavily from the pseudepigraphical writings attributed to Hermes Trimegistus, and some Christian mystics, such as the late Valentin Tomberg (1900-1973), have delighted in creatively combining the Christian gospel with the Western Hermetic tradition. Tomberg's magnum opus, *Meditations on the Tarot: A Journey into Christian Hermeticism*, is nothing short of magisterial, and is "must" reading for Christian mystics.

Can you summarize the Hermetic journey?

The Christian Hermeticist likens the spiritual process to *alchemy*. But instead of turning base metals into the gold, his goal is to transform himself into a sagely and illumined disciple. This involves the synthesis of four practices: *mysticism*, *gnosis*, *magic*, and *philosophy*. Mysticism represents the beginning of the Christian Hermetic journey, for without mysticism, contact with the Deity, there can be no such journey. Mysticism commences with Baptism by the Spirit. Once the disciple is baptized, "born again" (or from above), his practice of spiritual alchemy can begin.

Spiritual alchemy inaugurates with the "drinking" of Holy Water from above. As the Hermeticist grows in the Spirit, the "Water" turns into intoxicating "Wine," and then, finally, Holy Blood, mystical Elixir from on high. Thanks to the luminous Power of the Elixir, the Hermeticist is able to attain *gnosis* (high and deep spiritual knowledge) and master *philosophy* (the study of Reality and man's relation to it). This fusion of *mysticism, gnosis*, and *philosophy* equates to finding the fabled *philosopher's stone*. The Hermeticist not only employs the Power of the mystical Elixir to attain spiritual knowledge, he also utilizes it to practice sacred *magic*, the skillful blending of the Divine Will or Energy with his personal will and life-energy. This application of Divine Energy (the Power of the Elixir) toward the transformation and healing of self and others is akin to the practice of Indian *tantra* yoga. And like the tantric yogi, the Hermeticist's ultimate goal is union with the Deity. When the downpouring Holy Blood cracks open his Sacred Heart-center, untying the *Gordian Knot*, the Hermeticist's spiritual journey is over; he has found what he sought—the *Holy Grail*, Divine Union, the *Holy Chalice* filled, and overflowing, with eternal life-giving Blood from above.

Converting a Conventional Believer

How would you describe Christian mysticism to a bright but conventional Christian?

By explaining the mystical basis of the terms he's familiar with. For example, the term *Christian* means "little Christ"; hence, becoming a true Christian means *mystically* attempting to duplicate Jesus' realization. I'll go over the key terms, so you get the picture and can paint it for others.

Christianity begins with original sin, the fall from Grace. In other words, the root sin of humans is to fall (or retract) from *Grace*, God's Holy Spirit, or Blessing Power. A devout Christian recognizes and *confesses* his sin, and seeks *atonement* via *at-one-ment* with *Saving Grace*, God's *redeeming*, or soul-healing, Light-energy. The first time a Christian contacts (or is contacted by) Grace is called *baptism*, and when the experience is repeated, it is called *confirmation*. When the Christian's Sacred Heart-center is "cracked open" by the poured-down Spirit, and the *Sanctifying* Grace Flow becomes constant, he spontaneously realizes himself as a Christ, and like Jesus, his soul's Destiny is to dwell forever more in Heaven, the Divine Domain.

If your friend is a God-fearing, true-believer type, consider escalating the "Bad News"/"Good News" argument. First, tell him that unless he is truly *converted*—that is, willing to unconditionally submit, or at least attempt to submit, his whole person to God—then his destiny will be a cursed passage to *perdition* (Satan's infernal "outhouse"). If, on the other hand, he confesses his personal *deformation* and willingly undergoes *reformation* by *literally*, not figuratively, *conforming* himself to God's Will, the Holy Spirit, then the Kingdom of Heaven (the Lord's perpetual "Penthouse") awaits him.

My friend is an open-minded, scholarly type, not a fundamentalist.

Then describe the spiritual process in arresting intellectual terms to pique his curiosity. For example, employ a little Greek and tell him that *henosis* (union with the Holy One) is attained via the sacred processes of *katharsis* (psycho-physical purification), *kenosis* (self-emptying), *theosis* (divinization, or en-Light-enment, of the whole person), and *perichoresis* (interpenetration of the three persons, or hypostases). Tell him that real Christianity goes beyond *pleasure* (mindless *physical* enjoyment) and *joy* (uplifting *mental* association) and is about pure *bliss* (spontaneous *Spirit-full* happiness), which stems from a direct connection to the Holy Spirit, the Blessing/*Blissing* Power from on high. And when

Divine Union, *henosis*, is attained and *bliss* is realized as the very *nature* of one's own Christ Self, or *Beingness*, then, spontaneously, it morphs into *Beatitude*.

The Magical Mystery Tour

I've got a teenage friend into mind-expanding drugs—LSD, ecstasy, and ayawaska—but he has no interest in Christianity, which he equates with the brainwashed, puritanical, right-wing establishment. He knows from his drug experiences that there is more to existence than just the physical. How can I convert him to Eucharistic spirituality and get him off the drugs?

First, get him a copy of *Be Here Now*, by Baba Ram Dass. Ram Dass, along with fellow Harvard professor Timothy Leary (the famous countercultural drug guru), conducted extensive experiments with psilocybin and LSD in the 1960s. After years of experimentation, Ram Dass finally realized that drugs cannot produce en-Light-enment. He turned to Eastern spirituality and became the preeminent countercultural "salesman" for yoga and mysticism. The book is a very entertaining read, and, in fact, launched my "journey to the East" some forty years ago.

Second, forget an overtly Christian approach to spirituality for a rebellious young man who rightfully detests establishment "Churchianity." Instead, entice him with a *theurgical* (or magical/mystical) approach to en-Light-enment, which will likely jibe with his psychedelic drug experiences. Teach him how to contact the *Numinous*, and how, like a hierophant, or high priest, he can pull down Clear Light-energy. Once he learns how to pull down Clear Light-energy, the *Sambhogakaya*, or "Bliss Body," explain that the *Soma*, the intoxicating Ambrosial Flow he is channeling, is just another name for the Holy Spirit, and that the act of consciously connecting to it is equivalent to the practice of Holy Communion. If he's a thinker, a light will go off in his head, and he'll immediately realize that the essence of Christian mysticism, the Eucharist, is also the essence of all genuine religion, which is simply the practice of uniting one's individual consciousness with the *infinite* Spirit, which, when contacted, "expands" one's mind *infinitely* more than any drug can.

CHAPTER ELEVEN

Spiritual Literature: A Cognizant Overview

A Consideration of Mystical Texts

Beyond the Bible, what spiritual literature do you recommend for Christian mystics?

I've been reading spiritual books for more than forty years, and I maintain that wide and deep reading in other mystical traditions will greatly benefit Christian mystics. Disciples who expand their horizons beyond Christian mysticism will find a bounty of unique perspectives and insights relative to the en-Light-enment process in non-Christian sources. Although all the great mystical traditions, directly or indirectly, recommend the same spiritual practice—communion with Ultimate Reality, the Great Mystery—the degree to which each school succeeds in creating a clear and detailed "map" to the true "Holy Land," the Divine Domain, is debatable among spiritual pundits—and, as you'll see, I'm not the least bit shy about throwing my two cents in the ring and participating in the brouhaha.

I'll start with books on Christian mysticism and my favorite such text, *Meditations on the Tarot: A Journey into Christian Hermeticism*, by Valentin Tomberg. Simply put, this is an extraordinary account of the "perennial philosophy," filtered through the eyes of a sagely Catholic mystic. Although some of Tomberg's positions and perspectives are parochial (Christian-biased), the elaborate and affecting portrait he paints of the mystical Christian journey is both spellbinding and enlightening.

I seldom read a spiritual book more than once, but I've read Bernard McGinn's *The Foundations of Mysticism: Origins to the Fifth Century* three times, and I plan to read it again. Why? Because McGinn, a renowned theologian and historian, is immensely informative and engagingly readable. In this volume, McGinn doesn't limit himself to Christian mysticism, he examines mysticism in general and provides a deep, nuanced consideration of this challenging subject. Even though this is my second-favorite book on Christian mysticism, I only recommend it for intellectually inclined individuals.

Evelyn Underhill's *Mysticism*, first published in 1911, remains the classic general text on Christian mysticism. This volume provides not only an insightful analysis and overview of the Western mystical tradition and the mystical experience, but also passionate and inspiring prose from both Underhill and the mystics she examines. This book is "must" reading for students of Christian mysticism.

Although numerous Christian saints and sages throughout the ages have graced the world with spiritual teachings, in my opinion, the instructions of one, the inimitable Meister Eckhart, stand out above the rest. Eckhart, who comes across like a Zen master disguised as a fourteenth-century Dominican priest, specialized in radical apophatic (or "negative") mysticism, and his controversial sermons led to heresy charges against him. Although I don't embrace Eckhart's theology in toto, his sermons are "must" reading for serious students of Christian mysticism. The most comprehensive collection of Eckhart's sermons can be found in *The Complete Mystical Works of Meister Eckhart*. Unfortunately, this text is pricey (about $100), so if you're new to Eckhart, it might be a good idea to first sample his writings in less expensive translations and commentaries (which you can find at Amazon.com).

Beyond the four above-mentioned, highly recommended books, I am partial to three texts on Christian mysticism: 1) *The Mystic Christ*, by Ethan Walker (an inspiring, love-oriented consideration of Jesus' teachings from an Eastern mystical perspective); 2) *Inner Christianity: A Guide to the Esoteric Tradition*, by Richard Smoley (an intellectual, gnostic-oriented consideration of Christianity); and 3) *The Essential Writings of Christian Mysticism*, by Bernard McGinn (the definitive anthology of writings by the foremost Christian mystics throughout history). This book is valuable because the sample writings enable one to quickly and easily determine which mystics warrant further study.

Another category of Christian mysticism texts to consider is contemporary books that emphasize centering prayer (acquired contemplation). These books provide useful information and basic instructions for individuals looking to explore the Gospel's contemplative dimension. The foremost text in this category is *Open Heart, Open Mind*, by Thomas Keating. Another excellent book in this genre is *The Big Book of Christian Mysticism: The Essential Guide to Contemplative Spirituality*, by Carl McColman. McColman, who has been influenced by renowned integral philosopher Ken Wilber, is thoughtful and erudite, and his book offers a wealth of information on Christian mysticism and basic contemplation.

Now we'll move on to Hinduism. Although the two most popular Hindu spiritual traditions in the West are Raja Yoga (the Yoga Sutras of Patanjali) and Advaita Vedanta, the sharpest mystics hang their hat on Kashmir Shaivism, the acme of Indian spirituality. Because the central spiritual practice of Kashmir Shavism—Divine Communion and conductivity of the *Shakti* (Spirit)—is virtually identical to the esoteric Eucharist, I believe

Christian mystics can glean more insights from this tradition than any other Indian one. My suggestion is to start with *The Philosophy of Sadhana*, by Deba Brata SenSharma, and if you find Kashmir Shaivism to your liking, then consider the other books in this category on my Spiritual List (in the Appendix).

Although Kashmir Shaivism is my favorite Indian spiritual tradition, my favorite Indian guru, by far, is Ramana Maharshi (1879-1950), a *jnani* (or gnostic master) whose teachings are of the Advaita Vedanta variety. Every spiritual aspirant should at least sample this spiritual genius's teachings, and to this end, I recommend starting with *Be As You Are: The Teachings of Ramana Maharshi*, by David Godman. Every spiritual aspirant should also at least familiarize himself with Raja Yoga (in order to understand the basic principles of meditation), and a good introductory book to begin with is *How to Know God: The Yoga Aphorisms of Patanjali*, by Swami Prabhavananda and Christopher Isherwood. If you find Patanjali to your liking, upgrade to Swami Hariharananda Aranya's *The Yoga Philosophy of Patanjali*, a superb esoteric exegesis of the Yoga Sutras.

What Kashmir Shaivism is to Hinduism, Tibetan Dzogchen is to Buddhism: its highest teaching (and one that virtually mirrors the esoteric Eucharist, though from a nondualistic viewpoint). A good book to begin your investigation of Dzogchen with is *The Cycle of Day and Night: Where One Proceeds Along the Path of the Primordial Yoga: An Essential Tibetan Text on the Practice of Dzogchen*, by Namkhai Norbu. A wonderful, though challenging, second book to continue your investigation is the *Precious Treasury of the Way of Abiding*, by Longchen Rabjam. If Dzogchen is your cup of tea—and it is certainly mine—you will find numerous fine texts available on this wonderful trinitarian teaching. In addition to Buddhist Dzogchen texts, I highly recommend two other books on Buddhism: *Some Sayings of the Buddha, According to the Pali Canon*, by F.L Woodward, and *The Zen Teaching of Huang Po*, by

John Blofeld. The former is easily the finest general text on the Buddha's teachings, and the latter is regarded by many, including me, as the premier Zen book.

Beyond the esoteric core of the three major spiritual traditions— Christianity, Hinduism, and Buddhism—the Dharma that stands out is that of Adi Da Samraj (Adi Da, or Da, for short). Da, who founded his own religious organization, Adidam, was a fully en-Light-ened spiritual master and a great writer. His teachings, though somewhat derivative, are incredibly profound, and any spiritual seeker who ignores them does so to his own detriment. I personally have been greatly influenced by Da's teachings, and my writings clearly bear his "stamp." Because Da's teachings are all about *Satsang* (Divine Communion, or Relationship) and reflect his appreciation of Christian mysticism, they are particularly apropos for disciples of the Eucharist. I suggest starting with Da's autobiography, *The Knee of Listening*, moving on to *The Hridaya Rosary*, and then "graduating" with *The Pneumaton*.

I will conclude my recommendations with two books: *The First and Last Freedom*, by J. Krishnamurti, and *Objectivism: The Philosophy of Ayn Rand*, by Leonard Peikoff. Krishnamurti (1895-1986) and Rand (1905-1982) were both brilliant, free-thinking iconoclasts, and every serious Truth-seeker will benefit from studying their Dharmas. Though Krishnamurti was a mystic, and Rand an atheistic anti-mystic, their writings share a common denominator: both provide Truth-seekers with a cornucopia of unique philosophic insights.

How about Judaism and the Kabbalah? *You haven't mentioned any books from this tradition.*

I am Jewish by birth, and I wish there were some truly outstanding books on Jewish mysticism that I could *highly* recommend; but there are none—and believe me, I'm very aware of what's available in this genre. Yes, Gershom Scholem's *Major Trends in Jewish Mysticism* is a fine scholarly text, but it's not on the level of Bernard McGinn's *The Foundations of Mysticism.* And Moshe Idel's *Kabbalah*, while a noteworthy academic work, is hardly an inspiring mystical classic. I've examined the highly recommended Kabbalah books at Amazon.com, and to put it kindly, all of them are lacking. The *Zohar*, the foundational text of mystical Judaism, according to many, has been identified as inauthentic, as a forgery; and beyond that, it's simply not as good as the premier foundational texts of Buddhism and Hinduism. I believe that most people who read both the *Zohar* and the Hindu Bible, the *Bhagavad Gita*, would identify the latter as the superior text.

I don't want to leave the impression that there are no good books on Jewish mysticism; there are, and my Spiritual List recommends two of them: Scholem's *Major Trends in Jewish Mysticism* and *Jewish Meditation*, by Aryeh Kaplan. I just want to make it clear that I've yet to encounter a *great* Jewish mysticism text. Nonetheless, I believe that Jewish mysticism   because of its identification of the Sefirotic "Tree of Life" as the "map" of creation—has the potential to be the most integral, and therefore the foremost, school of mystical thought. But until a true kabalistic guru emerges, an en-Light-ened sage who can "read" the Sefirotic map from *both* the highest mystical and the deepest occult viewpoints, it's unlikely we'll see a truly outstanding Jewish mysticism text.

Your book recommendations seem weighted toward Christianity and don't exactly match the ones in Beyond the Power of Now.

These recommendations are geared toward Christian mysticism, because that's what we're considering. If we were focusing on, say, Tibetan Buddhism, I'd have suggested a few more Dzogchen texts and a few less Christian Mysticism ones. But the bottom line is simple: Concentrate your reading on the spiritual traditions that move you, but at least familiarize yourself with the top texts in the other great traditions.

CHAPTER TWELVE

Electrical Flesh, Electrical Bones

The Zen of Electrical Spirituality

Can you explain real meditation from an electrical energetic perspective? I've been a Zen practitioner for a long time, and I'd like to get a better understanding of my practice.

There are two major schools of Zen Buddhism—*Rinzai* and *Soto*. I predict that a third one will emerge in the future: *Electrical Zen*. It will emerge for one reason: Neither Rinzai nor Soto accounts for the electrical-like Energy (or Power) of spiritual life. Therefore, the door is wide open for a sharp Zen teacher to integrate the Holy Spirit into Zen.

In reality, the Holy Spirit, the *Sambhogakaya* in Mahayana Buddhism, is already one-third of the Buddhist Trinity—*Dharmakaya*, *Sambhogakaya*, and *Nirmanakaya*—but Zen, a reductionist, void-worshipping religious tradition, doesn't bother to acknowledge it. I speak knowledgeably about this, because I studied and practiced Zen for years.

So Zen needs to convert to Electrical Christianity?

No, Zen needs to convert to Electrical *religion*. The word religion is derived from the Latin word *religare*, which means to bind back to the Source. In reality, there is only one true religion or religious practice—Divine Communion. Divine Communion (called *Ati Yoga* or Dzogchen in Tibetan Buddhism) is simply the yogic practice of *yoking* one's soul (or *Nirmanakaya*) with the Spirit (or *Sambhogakaya*) in order to realize the timeless, spaceless God (or *Dharmakaya*).

The term Zen (*Ch'an* in Chinese) is derived from *Dhyana* (Sanskrit), which means *meditation*. And if Zen wants to promulgate the highest form of meditation, then it must acknowledge the practice of Electrical Spirituality (or Plugged-in Presence) as the direct, definitive way to the unborn, luminous Now.

What about the practice of koans (intense meditative focus on confounding, paradoxical questions)?

Original Zen meditation was all about letting go and detaching. If you read the early Chinese *Ch'an* Classics, such as *The Sutra of Hui Neng* and *The Zen Teaching of Huang Po*, all you encounter are endless directives to empty your mind, to cease grasping hold of concepts. But just surrendering or letting go, as I often point out, is an exclusive, reductive, low-energy practice, lacking the *conscious force*, or *spiritual voltage*, that a disciple needs to "break through" to the Other Side.

Because "declutching" alone is not an integral practice, the *Rinzai* school of Zen instituted the ultra-yang practice of *koans* to counterbalance the yin practice of self-emptying. But the mentally violent, self-torturous practice of koans, which Zen masters liken to "trying to smash one's fist through an iron wall," is unnecessary for a disciple who practices Plugged-in Presence, which *naturally* generates even more conscious force than koan meditation.

Plugged-in Presence, Holy Communion, generates *maximal conscious force* because it *is* consciousness itself plugged directly into the Source. Consciousness (or presence) + oneness = maximal conscious force. If Zen didn't devote itself to denigrating man's conceptual faculty, it would have figured out this en-Light-ening formula a long time ago.

Why doesn't Zen acknowledge the Holy Spirit?

Because Zen philosophy derives essentially from the Indian Mahayana Buddhist *Prajnaparamita Sutras*, which reduce everything to emptiness. Thus, any experience of any "object," even the Holy Spirit, or *Sambhogakaya*, is to be immediately voided. This anti-mind approach precludes Zen practitioners from understanding the trinitarian basis of spirituality and the role of Spirit in the en-Light-enment process. *Bodhicitta*, which means en-Light-ened Consciousness (or Conscious Light), is an important Mahayana Buddhist term, but Zen aficionados stare blankly at you when you mention Light-energy, or Spirit-force, as half of the Buddhahood project. The Mahayana Buddhist Trinity (*Dharmakaya*, *Sambhogakaya*, *Nirmanakaya*) mirrors the Christian one (Father, Holy Spirit, Son), but Zennists steadfastly ignore the *Sambhogakaya*, which would be like Christian mystics dismissing the Holy Spirit.

Zen Flesh, Zen Bones

In the Ten Ox Herding Pictures (Google for various interpretations), is the ox a metaphor for the Sambhogakaya, the Holy Spirit?

Yes. A disciple tames the wild bull, the *Shakti*, by becoming one with it. When the Zen disciple can indefinitely "ride" the now docile ox, he is well on his way to realizing his Buddha-nature. Some interpreters of these pictures consider the ox to represent one's Buddha-nature, but one's Buddha-nature can never be an object; it can only *be* the pure Subject. But when the empirical subject, the ego-self, unites with the Great Object, the reflected Light-energy of the One Mind, then he experiences his Buddha (or Self)-nature.

How about the thirty-two marks of a Buddha?

The thirty-two marks pertain to the physical characteristics caused by the *Sambhogakaya*, the Holy Spirit. The pressure, or force-flow, of the Divine Power literally transfigures the body, leaving common, recognizable effects. It's as if you start out spiritual life as a block of stone, and God, via his *Shakti*, "carves" you into a masterpiece with specific, identifiable characteristics.

How about Zen flesh and Zen bones?

Flesh represents the *Sambhogakayha*, the *fullness* or richness of the drawn-down Supernal Efflux. Bones represent *emptiness*. When a Zen disciple's self-emptying pulls down the *Sambogakaya*, suffusing his "bones" with Light-energy, then the union of Flesh and Bones produces Marrow, the penetrating realization of the *Dharmakaya*, the integral Truth Body that is God.

It sounds very intense.

It is. It's as if you're being cooked alive in the purgatorial Fire of God. In the Divine Cauldron, all distinctions melt into a single Intensity, and that Intensity is the very Force of Being. Once you're sufficiently "cooked," you "cool down" and rest in "the Bright," the blissful, radiant Light of Being.

There's no way to bypass the Fire?

As Adi Da put it, "The Fire must have its way. There is no Light without Fire…That is the Law."

Electrical Religion

Can you elaborate more on electrical religion and explain the energetic process of en-Light-enment?

First, a disclaimer: I have not cut the Sacred (or Mystic) Heart-knot, and thus I am not fully en-Light-ened. Consequently, my explanation will be provisional, not definitive. Nonetheless, I am a very advanced meditator, and I regularly rest in, and *as*, the Heart (or Christ Self) for protracted periods, and constantly channel intense *Shakti*, or Spirit Power. Furthermore, I am blessed/cursed with an ultra-sensitive psycho-physical vehicle that deeply feels, and enjoys/suffers, the effects of this electrical-like spiritual, or Kundalini, Energy. Therefore, I am able to describe this process as few others can. If I weren't able to feel this Power (or Energy) and its Ohm's Law (or electric-current)-like relationship to Presence (or Consciousness) and Poverty (or self-emptying), I wouldn't have been able to originate and develop my Electrical Spiritual Paradigm.

The core of my natal astrology chart (Scorpio Rising, with five planets in Cancer in the eighth house, including the Sun closely conjunct Uranus) signifies a karmic "destiny" (or extreme tendency) to profoundly, though painfully, experience Kundalini, Mother *Shakti*; and the rest of my chart (particularly Jupiter in Aries in the fifth house and Neptune in Libra in the eleventh house, opposite each other and squaring my Eighth house Cancer stellium) indicates a powerful desire to disclose and disseminate my *Shakti*-related insights. Eventually, I will write an autobiography detailing my forty-year "battle" with the Serpent Power, the "Coiled One" called *Kundalini*.

Now for the elaboration. When a yogi's conscious (plugged-in) presence is sufficiently intense (or unobstructed), the force (or pressure) that it generates awakens Kundalini (the dynamic power of the Divine). The "lower Kundalini" is initially experienced as intense energy rising up from the base of the spine to the crown. Eventually, this uncoiling, upward-rushing energy becomes permanently "polarized" toward the crown, and the periodic experiences of "rising ascent" subside. The yogi then experiences the energy as a constant upward force, as a current flow whose intensity varies according to his state of consciousness (meaning the conscious force, or voltage, he is generating, or the resistance he is releasing by self-emptying). The current's upward, "outward' pressure is particularly felt in the neck and the back of the head. It's as if the energy is seeking to escape from the "cage" of the physical.

The *ascended* spinal Kundalini leads a yogi to intense, absorptive *samadhis* (states of blissful, locked-in engrossment), but it cannot free him; only the "higher Kundalini" can. The higher Kundalini, the Holy Spirit, is the *descending* half of the Great Circuit, or Current, of the Divine. Whereas the "lower Kundalini" can be described as the "pushed up" power of *becoming spiritual* (which is the result of the yogi's own efforts), the higher Kundalini is the "pulled-down" Power of *Being Spirit-full* (which stems from Grace, the Blessing Flow from above). A smart yogi doesn't even involve himself with attempting to raise the lower Kundalini; instead, he simply focuses on connecting to the higher Kundalini, the Holy Spirit, and allowing its Light-energy to free, or en-Light-en, him.

The higher Kundalini, called *Shaktipat* in Hindu Kashmir Shaivism, descends down the frontal line of the body to the Sacred (or Mystic) Heart-center. The Heart, the immanent, indwelling Source, or Soul, functions like a vacuum cleaner, sucking the Spirit (as a current) down into itself. This "pulling" action of the Heart can be strongly felt in the third-eye area of the forehead. One's head can even violently jerk and twist from the force of this pulled-down Power, or "Spirit-invasion." When the Spirit-current reaches the Heart-center, the yogi experiences radiant warmth in the area just to the right of the center of his chest, and for a time, he abides in the blissful feeling of Being, as *Shakti* and *Siva* "dance" together in his irradiated Soul.

The descending Spirit-current doesn't stop at the Heart-center. Its presence, or pressure, can also be felt below it. For example, when I meditate, my solar plexus spontaneously contracts in response to the current. Likewise, the muscles along my spinal line and neck automatically tighten when I do my spiritual practice. I've been hooked up to a biofeedback machine with electrodes attached to my back and neck muscles. When I began to meditate, to utterly let go, my heart rate slowed, my blood pressure dropped, and, incongruently, my muscles contracted, sending the tension needle on the machine's meter to and beyond its highest reading, where it stayed as long as I maintained my disposition of effortless awareness. The doctors and technicians were flabbergasted. They had never seen the needle pulled to the end marking of the tension meter before, and they had no explanation for what they had witnessed. When I started talking about the Kundalini, their eyes glazed over, and I realized "modern" medicine wasn't ready for the "Coiled One."

Wow! Why does Kundalini make your muscles contract?

Muscles contract when exposed to an electric current, and the fact that mine contract in response to the Spirit-current led me to the correlation between electricity and spirituality. Then I started thinking about Ohm's Law and noticed that it seemed to apply to my conscious *presence* (as voltage), my ego *absence* (as ohms), and the Spirit-current (as amperage). It was a perfect dialectic, with *presence* as the thesis, *absence* as the antithesis, and the Spirit-current as the synthesis. And because of my background in spiritual philosophy, I was able to tie it in with the mystical teachings of the major religions—Christianity, Buddhism, Hinduism, and Judaism.

◈ ◈ ◈

How does Kundalini relate to Self-Realization?

Kundalini *is* the Self—in its dynamic phase or dimension. When the Kundalini is utterly free (or unconstricted), so is the Self. Ramana Maharshi, the great Hindu sage, said Kundalini is just another name for the Self. Just as the flames of a fire cannot be separated from the fire, the Kundalini action of the Self cannot be separated from the Self, one's Divine Beingness.

A Brief Theory of Electrical En-Light-enment

Can you explain the entire electrical en-Light-enment process relative to the body? You've described the descending and ascending currents, but I'm still not clear on how they relate to Light. All you've talked about are currents.

Again, this is provisional and basic, not definitive and detailed. It's based on my own spiritual experience, what I've read, and speculation. In the future, I expect great yogi-scientists to devote their lives to demystifying the physics and superphysics involved in the "en-Light-enment of the whole body" process. But for now, I hope my undeveloped thesis proves somewhat "enlightening."

When I view the body from an electrical spiritual perspective, I think of the Heart-center (or Soul-locus) as the source, or "battery," of a circuit, with the ascending and descending currents passing through, and infinitely beyond, the brain. The brain/mind functions as a "load" (a psycho-physical mechanism of resistance) that obstructs the circuit's current flow, causing the buildup of tension or pressure in the head and neck that advanced meditators typically experience. In an en-Light-ened being, the brain/mind "load" has been sufficiently altered or reduced, so as to allow the brain to function like a super light bulb, which emits a nimbus of light, or halo, which "hovers" above the crown.

Now a caveat: Even if this "battery model" is a reasonable facsimile of the Soul-Spirit nexus in a human being, an important distinction between the two must be made: Unlike the "battery model," the human Soul-Spirit is conscient and sentient; it is a knowing and feeling "entity." In other words, en-Light-enment of the bodymind can never be reduced to a "mechanical" or "scientific" description, no matter how accurate and elegant it may be.

When you talk about the brain/mind being a "mechanism of resistance," are you saying that thoughts impede the flow of the current through the brain?

That is correct. Thoughts modify and "shrink" consciousness, *contracting* it into a series of limited and bound states of consciousness. When consciousness (or voltage) is contracted, so is the current (or amperage). But you're barking up the wrong tree if you try to stop thinking. The point of real spiritual life is to outshine thoughts, not suppress them. The Light irradiates them before they can "shrink" your consciousness.

Now I'll answer your question about Light. The Spirit-current, like an electric current, produces a magnetic force field encircling it. In the case of the Spirit-current, the magnetic force field is called Presence or Light. The ancients knew about this Spirit-current and its correlation with the radiant, magnetic force field surrounding it, but because electricity had not yet been discovered, they had no way to explain it from a scientific perspective. One of the best allusions to this Spirit-Light relationship can be found in the Gnostic text *The Secret Book of John* (translated by Stevan Davies): "The Father looked into Barbelo [the pure Light surrounding the Invisible Spirit]... He stood in the Spirit's presence, and it was poured upon him."

Does the magnetic force field surrounding the Spirit-current come into play in a disciple's initiation?

Yes, it does. It's really a form of *induction* when a disciple enters the force field of a spiritual master. In such a charged space, the spiritual "transmission," or initiation, can take place with just a glance or a touch from the master. And if the disciple has already been initiated, the master's presence serves to intensify his *Shakti* flow. For those interested in more information on the subject of spiritual induction, I recommend the book *Pathways Through to Space*, by Franklin Merrell-Wolff (1887-1985).

If the Heart-center is like a battery, then it sounds like a Shaktipat *guru's functions can be likened to jumper cables, an outside power source that gets one's "spiritual engine" started.*

Good analogy. Just as it takes a threshold energy level to start a car, likewise it takes one to start one's spiritual life. When sufficient conscious force, either self-generated or guru-generated, is applied by, or to, an *aspirant*, then he is *initiated* by the Spirit. He becomes an *empowered disciple*, one who practices the Eucharistic discipline of Spirit Communion.

Jesus baptized his disciples with the power and presence of the Holy Spirit, or Holy *Ghost*; hence, he was called a *pneumatic*. But if Jesus were alive today, my guess is he would be referred to as a *spiritual electrician*, a divine Potentate, who, via his *Shakti*, "jump-starts," or baptizes, spiritual aspirants, thereby converting them to "true believers," *initiated conductors* of the Holy Spirit-current.

Beyond Ohm's Law: The Turning of the Wheel

What about the electrical power formula: P (Watts) = V (Voltage) x I (Amperage)? You haven't discussed watts relative to spirituality.

The webpage howstuffworks.com has a cool example of Ohm's Law and how it translates into the Power Formula:

> The three most basic units in electricity are voltage (V), current (I), and resistance (R). Voltage is measured in volts, current is measured in amps and resistance is measured in ohms.

> A neat analogy to help understand these terms is a system of plumbing pipes. The voltage is equivalent to the water pressure, the current is equivalent to the flow rate, and the resistance is like the pipe size.

> There is a basic equation in electrical engineering that states how the three terms relate. It says that the current is equal to the voltage divided by the resistance.

> Let's see how this relation applies to the plumbing system. Let's say you have a tank of pressurized water connected to a hose that you are using to water the garden.

> What happens if you increase the pressure in the tank? You can probably guess that this makes more water come out of the hose. The same is true of an electrical

system: Increasing the voltage will make more current flow.

Let's say you increase the diameter of the hose and all of the fittings to the tank. You probably guessed that this also makes more water come out of the hose. This is like decreasing the resistance in an electrical system, which increases the current flow.

Electric power is measured in watts. In an electrical system, power (P) is equal to voltage multiplied by current.

The water analogy still applies. Take a hose and point it at a waterwheel like the ones that were used to turn grinding stones in watermills. You can increase the power generated by the waterwheel in two ways. If you increase the pressure of the water coming out of the hose, it hits the waterwheel with a lot more force and the waterwheel turns faster, generating more power. If you increase the flow rate, the waterwheel turns faster because of the weight of the extra water hitting it.

This water analogy is particularly neat because the turning of the waterwheel is akin to the turning of the wheel (of Dharma) in Buddhism. Thus, when the Buddha initiated the first turning of the wheel at Deer Park in India to an audience of disciples, he was, in effect, transforming the electric "amperage" (or *Energy*) of the Spirit-current into the "wattage" (or *Power*) of Dharma transmission.

Although I loosely use the terms *Energy* and *Power* interchangeably, strictly speaking, they are not the same. Energy is simply the motion of something, and this motion can be chaotic: wasteful and unfocused. When energy is focused or organized, applied to a task, then it becomes power. For example, a light bulb's energy is measured in watts (or power) because the "wild" energy of the electrons in the current has been channeled into a specific task, that of making light. In the case of the Buddha, the "wild" universal *Shakti*, or Energy, was "tamed," and transformed into Dharma power, the first turning of the wheel.

There have been four turnings of the wheel in Buddhism: 1) *The Buddha's* original Dharma; 2) *Madhyamika's* emptiness Dharma; 3) *Yogacara's* Mind-only (or Buddha-nature) Dharma; and 4) *Vajrayana's* tantra Dharma. I predict there will be a fifth turning of the wheel: *Electrical Buddhism's* Plugged-in Presence Dharma.

Why will there be a fifth turning of the wheel? Because each turning after the Buddha's reflects one-third of Ohm's Law, and the fifth turning, Electrical Buddhism, will integrate those three plus the Buddha's into a unified whole. The first turning of the wheel, by the Buddha himself, set the wheel in motion; the second, by *Madhyamika*, emphasized emptiness (Poverty, or *Ohms*); the third, by *Yogacara*, accentuated Mind (Presence, or *Voltage*); and the fourth, by *Vajrayana*, focused on Energy (Power, or *Current*). The fifth turning will not only unify Buddhism, but also integrate it with Christianity.

Electrical Buddhism, Electrical Christianity

Is there any difference between Electrical Buddhism and Electrical Christianity?

No, they are just different names for the same practice. Electrical Spirituality subsumes both of them. There is no such thing as a Buddhist Truth, a Christian Truth, a Hindu Truth, or a Jewish Truth. There is only one Truth, and Electrical Spirituality is about realizing that Truth, exclusive of religious superstructures. It's fun to play with different Dharmas, to compare and contrast them—in fact, it's my favorite hobby—but unless you love

philosophy, there is no reason for you to become a scholar. All
you need to do is practice Plugged-in Presence—the Eucharist in
Christianity, and Dzogchen in Tibetan Buddhism. And if you're
incapable of doing this, then do mantra repetition or some other
basic form of meditation until you are.

Regarding the Spirit (or *Shakti*, or *Sambhogakaya*, or higher
Kundalini) and its electrical nature, all you need to know is that
it's a current of Blissful Energy, with a magnetic force field (of
invisible but palpable Light) surrounding it. All you need to do is
to connect to this Light-energy and allow it to en-Light-en you.
Be totally *present* (and plugged-in) and then utterly *absent*, so you
become a *conscious, but empty*, cup, ready to receive the Gift, the
poured-down Spirit, the electrical-like Bliss-current from above.

CHAPTER THIRTEEN

Electrical Psychology, Electrical Spirituality

Beyond Religion: Radical Psycho-Spirituality

Is there any reason to bring Jesus or religion into the discussion of self-liberation? If an individual creates his own bondage, why can't he create his own freedom? Why can't he skip the spirituality and just resort to psychology in order to free himself?

First off, "self-liberation"—freedom from craving and clinging—is only possible if one becomes Self-realized, which means awakening as a Christ or Buddha.

But such an awakening has nothing to do with the persons of Jesus or Buddha, who are, and always have been, superfluous to the en-Light-enment process. Innumerable beings throughout history have attained Self-realization (Christ Consciousness, or Nirvana) without having heard of Jesus or Buddha, and that alone proves they are unnecessary for self-liberation. The same thing that can be said about Jesus and Buddha can also be said about religions—that they are extraneous to en-Light-enment.

Bondage can be created; freedom can't. Freedom is always already the case; hence it can only be discovered (or unveiled). J. Krishnamurti, the renowned mystic, authored a book which I highly recommend: *First and Last Freedom*. The title's message is clear: Freedom cannot be attained, only lived.

Krishnamurti had no use for gurus, religion, or even the term "spirituality." His teachings of self-liberation could, perhaps, best be classified as "radical psychology." I used to attend Krishnamurti groups in San Diego in the '70s. I even traveled to Ojai, California, where Krishnamurti lived, to hear him speak. From my perspective at the time, no message could have been more liberating than his.

Krishnamurti's message, in a nutshell, is: practice effortless, choiceless awareness from moment to moment. This will free you from your self-created bondage and enable you to awaken "real intelligence." Although Krishnamurti occasionally alludes to a transcendent dimension, which he calls "the Highest," he never refers to it as Spirit and doesn't emphasize mystically uniting with it. Although in his journal, *Krishnamurti's Notebook,* he describes mystical experiences he calls "the Benediction," he doesn't direct spiritual seekers to seek this Blessing; instead, his focus, as always, is on understanding and obviating psychological conflict.

So Krishnamurti is the nuts when it comes to a radical psychological approach to self-liberation?

No, the late Adi Da (a.k.a. Franklin Jones, Bubba Free John, et al.) is. Da is Krishnamurti on 'roids. He audaciously claimed that he "cracked the cosmic code," and I say that anyone who can truly practice his "way of radical understanding" and fully grok his Dharma will accept his claim. According to Da, the ordinary (or un-en-Light-ened) man lives in a state of perpetual self-contraction, which is generated by his moment-to-moment activity of avoiding relationship (whole-person at-one-ment with life). A man's suffering, or *dis-ease*, is simply a reflection or symptom of this contraction; hence, any conventional "cure" (money, sex, drugs, entertainment, etc.) for the dis-ease is remedial, and never touches the *root* cause of the condition, the avoidance of relationship. Radical (or gone-to-the root) understanding is simply the enactment of the *asana* of Reality—conscious relationship—relative to life. And when this *asana*, or whole-bodily "posture," of conscious relationship is direct and unqualified, then, spontaneously, it morphs into perfect *nondual* Awareness and the feeling of Being. Anyone interested in a full elaboration of "radical understanding" should read Adi Da's *The Knee of Listening*, the greatest spiritual autobiography ever written.

The Elephant in the Ivory Tower

If this "radical understanding" is so great, why don't they teach it in psychology or philosophy courses at universities?

Universities are institutions of *lower*, not higher, learning. In my four years at the University of California, San Diego (1969-1973), putatively a top university, I never encountered a professor with an impressive mind. I encountered plenty of nerdy academics teeming with *exoteric knowledge*, but no wise men able to disseminate *esoteric wisdom*. The idea that any of these off-the-academic-assembly-line professors could, or would, teach radical understanding, is far-fetched, to say the least.

I liken university professors to blind men examining an elephant. Each professor gloms on to a part of the elephant, and on the basis of his experience (which may or may not accurately reflect a limited portion of the elephant), professes that "reality" to others. But because professors, like most everyone, have large egos, they commonly take their (right or wrong) insights about a portion of the elephant and extrapolate it to describe the whole elephant (the greater reality beyond their circumscribed experience).

The field of psychology provides us with a perfect example of the "blind men and the elephant" metaphor. First there was John B. Watson, the father of *behaviorism*, who couldn't find a brain in the elephant, so he declared, "consciousness doesn't exist," which reduced man to a glorified Pavlovian robot. Then there was Sigmund Freud, the originator of *psychoanalysis*, who, when he wasn't preoccupied with fondling his signature cigar, would grope the elephant and feel only a protruding, swollen appendage. Dr. Freud then informed the world that human reality can, in essence, be reduced to "penis consciousness," and that human spirituality, whatever form it might take, was no more than sublimated sexuality. Carl Jung followed Freud, and while he "touched" far more of the elephant than Freud, his mentor, he couldn't find a Self (Transcendental Consciousness) in the animal, so he decided that Transcendental (or Spirit-full) Consciousness was the same thing as the psychological "unconscious." I could continue to describe the forms of "blindness" that plagued the prominent psychologists who followed Jung, but I think you're quite capable of determining for yourself what parts of the elephant the various big-name post-Jung "shrinks" fixated on.

In short, modern psychology is a field littered with circumscribed, reductionist thinkers, men who see only the trees and not the forest. To put it pithily, the "shrunken" intellects of the "shrinks" have reduced psychology to an atomized, disjointed study of human cognition and behavior. Hence, we now need *Integral* Psychology to resurrect the fallen field of *disintegral* psychology.

Integral Psyche-ology

What's your vision of psychology and how it relates to spirituality?

My "vision" of psychology (the study of the soul, or *psyche*) is an integral one, but it differs markedly from New Age thinker Ken

Wilber's. Whereas Wilber, in his book *Integral Psychology*, attempts to integrate various schools of psychology into various matrices and an overarching hierarchical schema, my "integral" approach will be to consider the *psyche* (or soul) in the contexts of the three primary planes of existence—spiritual, physical, and psychical (or mental).

Because I haven't devoted myself to formulating or constructing a comprehensive, in-depth "Integral Psychology" per se, my "vision" will not be totally clear or intricately organized. In fact, it would probably take my writing a book on the subject for me to fully develop it. Nonetheless, I believe my embryonic "vision" will provide positive direction and useful insights for anyone interested in the field of integral psychology.

I'm going to call my "vision" *Integral Psyche-ology*, because I believe that integral psychology is about the holistic study of the *psyche*, the *living* soul. And because the dynamic nature of the soul is spirit, *living* energy, I maintain that any "integral" study of the psyche *must* account for its correlative spirit-energy. Moreover, because the human soul—at least in a given lifetime—is encased within a physical body, any integral, or holistic, consideration of the psyche must also be *psycho-somatic* in nature: that is, incorporate the corporeal into the study. And, of course, any consideration of the soul must also attempt to decipher it psychically: that is, to analyze its root psychical "structure," which is composed of myriad mental-emotional seed tendencies.

Now, let's start our consideration of Integral Psyche-ology with the psychical deciphering of the soul itself. An individual's "soul-matrix" (the composite of psychical seed tendencies that "sprouts" as his mind and emotions) is located in his Sacred (or Mystical) Heart-center, just to the right of the center of his chest. Hindu yogis call this Heart-center the *Hridayam,* and it is distinct from the *anahata heart chakra* in the *sushumna*, the central nadi, or subtle-body nerve channel. I'm not going to waste my time trying to prove this is true. You can only prove it to yourself, yogically. But it is my experience and that of many revered sages, including, most notably, Ramana Maharshi, India's greatest guru in the twentieth century.

When one's psychical seed-tendencies, which the Hindu yogis call *samskaras*, "sprout," instantaneously rising up from the *Hridayam* (the Heart, or Soul, "center") to one's brain via *Amrita Nadi* (the non-physical yogic channel connecting the soul and the brain), then the psychical seed-tendencies crystallize as impulses, desires, and thoughts. Embodied consciousness, the individual soul, is located in the Heart-center, and the brain is the organ or mechanism through which this consciousness functions as mind.

I second Plato's tripartite vision of the soul (cognitive, conative, and affective), and the psychical seed-tendencies reflect various admixtures of these three soul "elements." The seed-tendencies "hook up" in manifold concatenations in the soul, and the resulting psychical formations translate into identifiable impulses, desires, and thoughts via the brain. I don't want to get sidetracked into a lengthy, technical elaboration on the complex "seed-to-thought" (or soul-to-brain) mechanism, so I'll move on to the "deciphering" of one's soul, the process of psychological self-understanding.

Psychological Self-understanding and Holistic Healing

Ken Wilber acknowledges the *enneagram* (a ninefold typology of personality types), but not astrology, as a means to psychological self-understanding. Unbeknownst to Wilber, the enneagram is derived from astrology, which subsumes and transcends it as a system of human classification and understanding. The nine enneagram types mirror the "qualities," "traits," or "energies" of the first nine astrological planets — Sun, Moon, Mercury, Venus, Mars, Jupiter, Saturn, Uranus, and Neptune. Pluto is missing because the enneagram originated prior to the discovery of Pluto in 1930. Consequently, even on a superficial level, the enneagram is an incomplete tool for self- and other-understanding. But because Wilber is partially buried in the very zeitgeist "flatland" he heavily criticizes, he buys into the *conventionally acceptable* enneagram while rejecting the far more complete *occult* oversystem of astrology, from which it derives. Wilber rejects astrology because various studies have found it an ineffective predictive tool. But the findings of these studies are not surprising, because the "stars" only impel, they do not compel. Person-centered astrology, which holistically oriented astrologers practice, is not about fortune telling; it is about deciphering psychical tendencies. And because these tendencies are contextual— existing within a particular human being who is a product of unique heredity and social conditioning—an astrologer can only be effective when he considers a chart integrally: that is, relative to a whole person. Such an "integral" consideration elevates astrology from a "horizontal" (conventional or flat) typology to a "vertical," or multi-level, tool of self- and other- understanding. Moreover, it enables a psychologist to apply it to almost any field of psychology, such as humanistic, cognitive, sociocultural, psychodynamic, and learning.

Astrology is a nonpareil tool for deciphering the soul-matrix, the blueprint or map of an individual's *karma*, or inborn seed-tendencies, which manifest as his personality and life-energies. A competent professional astrologer can teach a client far more about himself—his personal strengths and weaknesses and areas of harmony and disharmony—than any conventional psychologist. Even the Myers-Briggs personality types, which Ken Wilber acknowledges in his Integral Psychology, can be subsumed under astrology. The four fundamental personality types in Myers-Briggs—feeling, sensation, intuition, thinking—correlate almost exactly with the four astrological elemental types—water, earth, fire, and air. For example, if an individual has the majority of his astrological planets in Cancer, a water sign, his primary mode of interfacing with the world will be via the function of feeling. As a long-time professional astrologer, I could write volumes about astrology and its relation with psychology, but, again, I don't want to go off on a long tangent. So, all I will say here is that mainstream psychology has badly missed the boat by not utilizing astrology as a tool for soul-understanding, or psyche-ology; and to my mind, any practice of psychology that doesn't include astrology cannot be considered "integral."

Astrology doesn't just provide insight into one's mind and personality; it's also a source of information about one's body and physical constitution. But an even better tool for "reading" the human body is *iridology* (or *iridiagnosis*), analysis of the physical vehicle via examination of the iris, which reflects the inborn strengths and weaknesses and current condition of one's body—organs, glands, nervous system, et al. Because a human being is a body-mind complex, a person's body and mind are inextricably linked. Consequently, when an iridologist examines an individual's iris, he sees not only his body, but to an extent his mind, reflected particularly in his inborn constitution and the current condition of his brain and nervous system. For example, if the iridologist notes heavy "pressure" on a particular region of the brain, indicated by markings in the iris, he'll know that the person has an ego problem and functions under extreme stress.

Iridology is by no means the only modality for "reading" the constitution and current condition of the body (and its relation to the mind), but to my knowledge, it is the best. An integral holistic healer, which is what a general psychologist (or "soul doctor") should be, could also incorporate other tried-and-true tools of diagnosis, such as Indian Ayurveda, into his repertoire, and thus be able to obtain an even more complete picture of a client's psycho-physical state. And if a consideration of astrological transits (the current position of the planets relative to one's natal chart) were added to the mix, then the healer would have an integral picture of the client's body-mind condition and could recommend an appropriate holistic regimen to rejuvenate and balance his organism. Such a regimen would likely incorporate diet, herbs, and bodywork (including "gross-body" practices such as massage and chiropractic, and "subtle-body" ones such as acupuncture and Jin Shin Jyutsu).

The Soul as Energy

Now that we've considered the soul from a psycho-physical perspective, we'll look at it from an energetic one. The common occult term for "soul-matrix" is "astral body," and the astral body (the repository of one's psychical seed-tendencies) has an energetic correlate or dimension called the *etheric body*, which permeates the physical body and, as an *aura*, extends, or emanates, beyond it. When a psychic "reads" a person's aura, she, in effect, is reading his soul.

The soul *is* consciousness, and consciousness *is* energy. Therefore, the freer a man's consciousness is, the more radiant is his aura. The ordinary man's soul, or consciousness, due to his incessant grasping (or clinging and craving), is in a chronic state of contraction; thus his aura, or etheric body, is less than pristine and shining.

If psychology is to be truly integral, or "soul-full," it must account for the existence of, and correlation between, a man's astral and etheric bodies. Moreover, it must also explain this correlation in a relational context—the interdynamics involved when the astral and etheric bodies of one individual interact with those of another. And only astrology, via its "map" or "blueprint" of a person's astral body (or psychical matrix), provides graphic insight into the intrinsic chemistry and energy involved when the soul (or consciousness "structure") and spirit (energy emanating from the soul) of one person interact with those of another. Hence, until and unless psychology embraces astrology, it will remain in the dark when it comes to understanding the "chemistry" and "superphysics" involved in interpersonal relationships.

But it isn't enough for psychology to understand intra-and interpersonal astral-etheric dynamics; for it to be truly integral, its practitioners must also be able to teach people the Way to free their souls—and the Way to this salvation is the Eucharist, the practice of Holy Communion, or Plugged-in Presence. This practice pulls down Spirit Power, which irradiates one's psyche, thereby allowing one's soul to "expand" (or de-contract) and thereby shine through and beyond its physical encasing, the body. This pulled-down Spirit Power, or Saving Grace from above, is a man's only true salvation. And an integral psychologist, or holistic "soul doctor," will prescribe this "medicine," and no other, to free the souls of his patients from their root suffering, the self (or soul)-contraction.

So an integral psychologist could teach Holy Communion to a Christian and the same practice to an atheist, but just call it Plugged-in Presence.

Yes. And once the atheist awakened pulled-down Power, the living Spirit, he would no longer be an atheist.

You say freedom cannot be attained—that it is always already the case. But you also say that that one's soul must be divinized by the Spirit before one can awaken and be free. This seems like a contradiction.

Your True Nature, or Christ Self, is always already free, so in that sense this freedom cannot be attained—but you cannot realize this Self-freedom until you crack open the Heart-knot tying off, or "imprisoning," your inner Splendor. And only Grace, the Holy Spirit, can untie the Heart-knot and set you unconditionally free, as the splendorous Self.

Even in religions like original Buddhism, where the Holy Spirit isn't explicitly mentioned, its action is implicit. For instance, in the *Pali Canon*, the standard scriptures of the Theravada tradition, the Buddha equates the attainment of Nirvana with what he terms the "Heart-release." For any kind of knot to "release" there must be *action*—and the only action that can open the Heart is that of the Spirit. In fact, if you read Theravada Buddhist scriptures, you will repeatedly see the Buddha referred to as "the Blessed One." Well, if he is the "Blessed One," what has "Blessed," or is "Blessing," him? The Same Holy Spirit that Blessed Jesus and which Blesses all other great mystics. And when Mahayana Buddhism developed from Theravada Buddhism, the Holy Spirit (or Ghost), which the Mahayanists term the *Sambhogakaya*, became part of the Buddhist Triple Body (*Trikaya*), which mirrors the Christian Trinity.

Radical Psycho-Spirituality versus Holy Communion

Why don't you teach radical understanding instead of Eucharistic spirituality?

For two reasons: First, only rare individuals are capable of practicing it. Second, why dispense with the wonderful mystical teachings of Christianity, which emphasize Grace and devotion? Most people want a spiritual practice that includes the warmth and affection of a personal relationship with the Deity, and mystical Christianity provides this. Even though I teach *gnostic*

Electrical Christianity, I do so as a supplement to devotional communion. All are free to practice pure gnostic connectedness, but most prefer devotionally worshipping the Spirit and receiving its Blessing Power. And so that is what I emphasize in my teaching.

I like the idea of being able to turn my atheist friends on to Plugged-in Presence and Ohm's Law and my Christian friends on to Eucharistic spirituality.

That's the right attitude, one that enables a disciple to convert most anyone to the practice of Divine Communion. Open-minded Christians will love learning a method to commune with the Holy Spirit; Buddhists will dig Plugged-in Presence because it's really mindfulness on 'roids, mindfulness elevated to Mind-*full*-ness; and guys into science will be intrigued with the idea of applying Ohm's Law to "expand" their consciousness.

CHAPTER FOURTEEN

The Spiritual Politics of Jesus

Jesus' Politics and the Federal Reserve

If Jesus were alive today, would he be political or apolitical?

That's a good question, and no one knows for sure. Arguments can be made for either possibility. One could argue that he would be apolitical because his focus was not on this world, but on heaven. As Jesus himself put it: "My kingdom is not of this world." And as the "Prince of Peace," some of his actions seem to imply surrender to government authority. For example, when confronted with the question of whether it was lawful for Jews to pay taxes to Caesar, his response, "Render unto Caesar the things which are Caesar's, and unto God the things that are God's" (Matthew 22:21), can be construed as an enjoinder to submit to secular law.

But I'm going to argue that Jesus would be very political if he were alive today. In fact, the more I've contemplated the question of Jesus' politics, the more convinced I've become that he would be outspokenly political if he were spreading his Gospel now.

Would he be a Democrat, as Barack Obama believes?

Hardly. I think the last thing Jesus would support is Big Brother and the Nanny State. In fact, I think he would positively rail at the neo-Marxist fascism of Obama and his Democratic brethren.

But the Republican politicians—except for Ron Paul and a few others—are no better; in fact, they may be worse because they reek of hypocrisy and thus are wolves in sheep's clothing. Bush Jr. may be the worst president in U.S. history, and he begat Obama, maybe the second worst.

What Biblical support do you have for your thinking?

Let's start with Jesus' "Render unto Caesar" statement. A superficial consideration of this statement would lead one to conclude that Jesus favors capitulation to secular authority, even if it is evil in nature like the Roman Empire. But as sharp analysts point out, Jesus doesn't consider the money or property owned by individuals to belong to the State (Caesar in this case). Consequently, his statement, which is a clever response to a baited question by a Pharisee, is in no way a vote for paying unjust taxes to an evil empire. Given the current immorality and dysfunction of the U.S government, I seriously doubt if Jesus, à la Warren Buffett and Stephen King, would be clamoring for higher taxes on the rich. Instead, I believe, he would be pushing to get rid of the IRS, an abominable "service" if ever there was one.

Even though Jesus promotes non-materialism—"Again I tell you, it is easier for a camel to go through the eye of a needle than for a rich man to enter the kingdom of God" (Matthew 19:24)—his actions and statements throughout the Bible make it clear that he believes in private property and capitalism. In the parable of the workers in the vineyard (Matthew 20:1-16), for example, he demonstrates his free-market bias and respect for privately owned businesses. When the last worker who showed up an hour before quitting time was paid the same as those who worked all day, Jesus tells the all-day workers to quit complaining because they were treated fairly according to the terms of their individual contracts.

In addition to being a free-market advocate, Jesus also stumps for honest money, a sound currency. The fact that he threw the thieving moneychangers out of the temple indicates that if he were around now, he would likely direct his bile at the United States Federal Reserve, the biggest scam and largest counterfeiting ring in history. The truth is, the "Federal" Reserve isn't even federal; it's just the private banking cartel—the "Banksters"—controlling and manipulating the U.S. and world economy, while enriching themselves and the ruling elite in the process.

So the term "Federal Reserve" is a misnomer, and this agency is just the modern, institutionalized version of the Biblical moneychangers?

Sad but true. By indiscriminately "printing money" and putting it into circulation, the Federal Reserve increases the money supply, which causes inflation, which devalues the dollar. The only word for this is *stealing*. The fact is, since the U.S. went off the gold standard in 1971, the U.S. dollar has lost eighty percent of its value against the Swiss franc. Moreover, thanks to the Federal Reserve's oft-ill-timed lowering of interest rates, the U.S. economy has suffered from burst bubbles in the stock and housing markets, and now, as I write this in 2012, it is in critical condition, on life-support in the form of various government stimulus programs.

I do not believe that Jesus would tolerate the current state of U.S. financial affairs. Just as he threw the moneychangers out of the temple, he would likely attempt to do the same to the "Federal" Reserve, the *private* Banking Cartel in drag. In his book *Secrets of the Temple: How the Federal Reserve Runs the Country*, author William Greider details the omnipotence of the Fed.

Jesus, never tolerant of corrupt money practices, would likely expose the Fed's shenanigans to the masses, and a revolution on some level would doubtless ensue.

◊ ◊ ◊

Why isn't the Federal Reserve held accountable for its actions?

They're not even audited, so they can print money as they see fit, distribute it to their banker buds, and even bankrupt the country in the process—all without being held accountable. Congress has never held them accountable because ninety percent of its members are too stupid or corrupt to care. If I said what I really think about our federal government, the bastards would probably lock me up in one of America's new, nationwide FEMA camps (Google the term for details), and no one would ever hear from me again. I'm not ready for martyrdom just yet, so I take care to bite my lip and tone down my rhetoric.

Fascism and Marxism, Alive and Well in America

How could the government lock you up for just exercising free speech?

With the passage of the National Defense Authorization Act (NDAA) in 2011, the government can now, on a whim, indefinitely detain any U.S. citizen they consider a threat to "national security." They don't have to prove you're guilty of a "crime," and you have no right to an attorney or a trial. On top of the NDDA, President Obama, in 2012, signed the National Defense Resources Preparedness Executive Order (NDRP), which builds upon the NDAA and puts the government completely above the law, giving them unchallengeable control of virtually every aspect of American life whenever they deem it "necessary." With the passage of the NDAA and NDRP Acts on top of the already-in-place Patriot Act, America has "officially" become a fascist state.

But it's unconstitutional for the government to detain citizens without access to legal counsel and a fair trial.

The goal of Obama is to subvert the Constitution and transform America into a quasi-Marxist state. George Bush called the U.S. Constitution "just a piece of paper," but Obama wants to go an extra step and burn the "piece of paper." The term "Marxism" is a no-no among Obama Democrats because it, rightfully, has negative connotations. So they euphemistically refer to themselves as Progressives and, disingenuously, disavow any allegiance to Karl Marx's *Communist Manifesto.*

I'm confused. You're labeling Barack Obama both a fascist and a Marxist, but fascism is extreme right-wing while Marxism is extreme left-wing. How can he be both?

You've been bamboozled by political bullshit. But you're hardly alone. In fact, in 1970, when I studied Marxism at UCSD under the iconic neo-Marxist professor Herbert Marcuse, I too was led to believe that fascism was a "right-wing" phenomenon, the polar opposite of "left-wing" Marxism. But many years later, when I finally read Ayn Rand, my political "savior," I learned that fascism, like Marxism, is left-wing, and *statist*, in nature. In other words, fascism and Marxism are two closely related variants of *collectivism.* If you're interested in political truth, you *must* read Rand. For now, here are a few excerpts from *The Ayn Rand Lexicon* that will clarify the *non-distinction* between Marxism (or communism, or socialism) and fascism:

> Fascism and communism are not two opposites, but two rival gangs fighting over the same territory... both are variants of statism, based on the collectivist principle that man is the righteous slave of the state.

A statist system—whether of a communist, fascist, Nazi, socialist, or "welfare" type—is based on the... government's unlimited power, which means: on the rule of brute force. The differences among statist systems are only a matter of time and degree; the principle is the same. Under statism, the government is not a policeman, but a legalized criminal that holds the power to use physical force in any manner and for any purpose it pleases against legally disarmed, defenseless victims.

The difference between [socialism and fascism] is superficial and purely formal, but it is significant psychologically: it brings the authoritarian nature of the planned economy crudely into the open.

The main characteristic of socialism (and of communism) is public ownership of the means of production, and, therefore, the abolition of private property. The right to property is the right of uses and disposal. Under fascism, men retain the semblance of pretense of private property, but the government holds total power over its use of disposal.

The dictionary definition of *fascism* is: "a government system with strong centralized power, permitting no opposition or criticism, controlling all affairs of the nation (industrial, commercial, etc.), emphasizing an aggressive nationalism..." (*The American College Dictionary*, New York: Random House, 1957).

Let's consider what Rand says. She emphasizes that a *statist* system (what America has morphed into from an *individualist* nation) is, like Caesar's Rome, based on "unlimited power" and "brute force." This is the opposite of what Jesus, the Prince of

Peace, stands for. Jesus subscribes to the dictum *Do no harm*, which means, *do not initiate force against a person, or steal their property*. This is the libertarian, *individualist* credo that America was founded on. It is directly, and irreconcilably, contrary to what Obama, a fascist-socialist, stands for and does. And yet, Obama has the audacity to claim Jesus was a Democrat. But given that Obama considers himself, and refers to himself as, a black man when he is really a mulatto, it's not the least surprising that he is also confused about Jesus' political identity.

But the Democrats believe in Christian-type charity, helping the poor and needy.

When a corrupt Robin-Hood type government (which takes out a HUGE middleman's cut) robs Peter to pay Paul, that is legalized theft, not charity. Charity is *you* deciding whom you want to give your money to. Jesus never recommended the government as the answer to anything, least of all charity.

Liberals versus Conservatives

You've ragged on the Democrats. How about the Republicans?

You mean the *Republicrats*. They're actually the flip side of the same coin as the *Democans*. Whereas the Democrats want to control, actually own, *your* money, the neocons, the mainstream Republicans, focus on controlling your personal life, on saving you from a life of "sin." These brainwashed moralists invariably pledge firm allegiance to the Constitution and the ideal of liberty, but yet these two-faced hypocrites want to dictate how you live your personal life. They champion grossly wasteful, ineffective government programs, even "wars," against drugs, gambling, pornography, and prostitution without realizing that Jesus would want no part of their social fascism, their obsessive legislation of "morality." For example, in John, Chapter 8, Jesus intercedes when a prostitute is about to be stoned to death for her sexual "sin." He challenges the accusers, stating: "Let he who is without sin cast the first stone." As the accusers slink away, Jesus instructs her to go and "sin no more." Clearly, as his actions demonstrate, Jesus is anything but a social conservative.

It seems as if Jesus was a libertarian in every way. Do you think he would be a supporter of the Ron Paul Revolution?

Given his ideals and values, I believe he would be. But if Jesus' support seemed to ensure Paul's, or another libertarian's, election as president, the Powers that Be would likely assassinate both of them. There's no way they'd allow a libertarian to rain on their fascist parade. Because they were able to cast Paul as your "crazy uncle," he was nothing more than a nuisance. But if a libertarian candidate's election seemed imminent, then you'd better believe they'd be thinking about taking him out.

It seems as if there's no real choice between liberals and conservatives. It's like trying to choose between a rock and a hard place.

Here's my analysis of conservatives and liberals: The typical social conservative, such as Rick Santorum or Michele Bachman, is a Bible-thumping idiot. These brain-dead, dark-age moralists oppose readily available contraception because it "leads to sex." They believe the Earth is six thousand years old, and think wearing a suit and tie to church reflects real religious values and garners God's grace. They believe in Manifest Destiny, that God has chosen the U.S. to rule the world, which justifies massive military spending and an aggressive, imperialist foreign policy.

The typical elite, or "chosen," liberal, such as Barack Obama, Bill Clinton, or Al Gore, is a product of either Harvard or Yale, and as such, is a hubris-filled, left-wing "social engineer" who believes he is uniquely endowed to inject "progressive" socialist programs into the American "bloodstream." He is a facile pragmatist who thinks he can, like a master chef, combine Marxism, capitalism, and corporatism into an integral brew, and then spread this concoction around the globe in the form of a "New World Order." But in reality, he is just as brainwashed as Santorum or Bachman—but in this case it is the academy, the Ivy League "church," that has "programmed" his brain, filling it with secular dogma that is socialist and statist in nature. The curricula at these elite academies have to be socialist and statist (or essentially neo-Marxist) in nature because these institutions of "higher learning" are producing the "leaders" of the "free world," and these leaders must lead via a program of "progressive social-engineering." Why must they lead via such a program? Because the New World Order Ruling Elite—the international banking cartel (the "Banksters) and the giant multinational corporations—say so. They insist on politicians who will partner up with them and help them create the Global Corporate State, a New World Order that reflects just the right combination of Marxism, capitalism, and fascism to meet their totalitarian needs.

Since Ronald Reagan left office, Harvard and Yale have taken over the American presidency. George Bush, Sr., is a Yale graduate, and his successor, Bill Clinton, attended Yale Law School. After Clinton's two terms, George Bush, Jr., another Yale product, defeated, first, John Kerrey, a Yale graduate, in 2000, and then Al Gore, a Harvard man, in 2004. After Bush's two terms, Barack Obama, a Harvard Law School graduate, was elected President in 2008. And the 2012 presidential election pitted Obama against a fellow Harvard product, Mitt Romney.

Is this Harvard-Yale domination of the presidency just a coincidence? Not in my book. I firmly believe that the Global Elite, via their arm, the Bilderberg Group (a network of executives from the leading multinational corporations and top national politicians who meet annually to consider jointly the immediate and long-term problems facing the West), has a special relationship with these schools, and they choose particular individuals from them in order to satisfy their agenda. I believe that Barack Obama was one of these chosen individuals, and that the Bilderberg Group was instrumental in his election as president in 2008.

But the Democrats are supposed to be the party of the common people; they're supposed to protect us against the tyranny of Corporate America.

That's like asking the fox to guard the chicken coop. In reality, the Democrats, just like the non-libertarian Republicans, are fully in bed with Corporate America. The majority of Washington politicians have sold their souls to these special interests, and their real goal is to do their bidding, not to protect the common man. This marriage between government and big business is called "crony capitalism," a genteel term for fascism. In short, the Republican Party represents *conservative fascism*, and the Democratic Party *liberal fascism*. Jesse Ventura's book *DemoCRIPS and ReBLOODicans*, an entertaining as well as enlightening read, properly exposes the two mainstream political parties as Mafia-like gangs, as giant protection rackets intent on eliminating any upstart political movement that threatens their exclusive power and control.

But the Democrats claim that if a free-market libertarian like Ron Paul became president, the unregulated corporations would run roughshod over the people.

If that's true, then why didn't Corporate America and Wall Street back Ron Paul? Because Ron Paul didn't offer them special favors, *corporate welfare*. He was against the bailouts and believes in separation of economy and state as well as separation of church and state. When economy and state are not separate, you no longer have true, or free-market, capitalism; instead, you have crony capitalism: the corporate state, fascism.

If what you're saying is true, why don't the people vote for Ron Paul and other libertarians, and end the tyranny?

The common man has been brainwashed by either, or both, the mainstream Church and the leviathan State (via its public education system). Then, when he gets home from work every day and turns on the TV, all he gets is Corporate Propaganda, in one form or another. Consequently, unless he's a rare independent thinker, he's going to be firmly enmeshed in the Matrix, and be no more than just another programmed human robot (though part of his programming will be to convince him he's a free thinker). Consequently, he won't comprehend that the U.S. Government has effectively been privatized, and is really just the legal Mafia, devoted to enriching and empowering itself at his expense. Unable to think outside the Establishment-imposed box, he'll mindlessly vote for either an establishment Democrat or Republican, and ignorantly dismiss libertarians faithful to the U.S. Constitution as "extreme."

Democracy is a Dirty Word

What's the most important political fact that Americans need to learn?

That the American system is *not* a democracy, it is a *constitutional republic*. "Democracy" means unlimited majority rule. An example of democracy is two wolves and a sheep voting on what they'll have for dinner. Democracy denies individual rights. Simply put, it is a form of totalitarianism, forced submission to the will of a group. Democracy is fine for certain functions, such as electing personnel, but it must be a subordinate system, subsumed under the principles of constitutional republicanism.

But even George W. Bush, a Republican president, constantly referred to America as a democracy, and never as a republic.

That's why I call "fascist" neoconservatives like Bush: Republi*crats*. Bush, like Obama, is a mere puppet or tool of the New World Order gang, which has no interest in awakening the brainwashed masses, the "sheeple," to the *fundamental* principle of constitutional republicanism, meaning the principle of *inviolable* individual rights that the State cannot abrogate. Hence, George W., at the behest of the Powers that Be, devoted his presidency to the imperialist mission of spreading statist, or *fascist*, democracy around the globe.

The Four "Quadrants" of Integral Politics

Ken Wilber, the renowned integral philosopher, explains political systems and philosophies via a four-quadrant model and eight-level "spiral dynamics" hierarchy. According to spiral dynamics, the Ayn Rand and libertarian viewpoints that you're espousing are only at level five of the eight-level political-evolutionary hierarchy. What's your response to this?

Ken Wilber is an avant-garde thinker worth reading and considering. But although he unearths fertile new ground, he doesn't dig very deep into the soil; hence, his spiritual and political writings are less than profound and not truly "integral." I don't want to go off on an involved tangent, since many of you are unfamiliar with Wilber's writings and political philosophy, so

I'll just quickly summarize my major criticisms of Wilber's Integral Politics for those of you interested in the subject.

First off, levels seven and eight of the spiral dynamics evolutionary political hierarchy that Wilber subscribes to are a complete joke—totally vague and nebulous New Age mumbo jumbo. I won't waste my time or yours attempting to deconstruct this inchoate crap. Second, Wilber and spiral dynamics display their strong left-wing bias in level six. This level includes "post-modernism, egalitarianism, multiculturalism, subjective thinking, and decision-making through *consensus*." Postmodernism is utter drivel. The fact that Wilber gives any credence to this anti-philosophy is a black mark on his work. The placement of some of the other philosophies and/or orientations I've listed from level six bespeaks of a collectivist or liberal-fascist, mindset. For example, "egalitarianism" and "multiculturalism" exemplify reduc-tionism rather than integralism, because instead of emphasizing equal individual rights and opportunity for all citizens, they focus attention on special-interest groups rather than on the *whole*—the organic "melting pot" that a truly free America would naturally be. Finally, the core description of level six—"Sacrifice self-interest now in order to gain acceptance and group harmony"—could be the mantra for any communist or fascist state. I'm sure Hitler's Nazi party would have merrily chanted it, because my late father, a German Jew who escaped from Germany in 1936, told me as much. In sum, it is farcical to place the various spiral dynamics "sixth-level" philosophies and orientations above Rand's "fifth-level" Objectivism."

I think you're being unfairly critical of Wilber, who is a very positive New Age influence. He thinks globally and wants to bring about an integral world.

The international banking cartel, the Bilderberg group, and multinational corporations, like Monsanto, have beaten Wilber to the punch when it comes to creating an "integral" New World Order. While Wilber talks the talk, they walk the walk. I just hope he appreciates their Orwellian efforts when they tell him it's time for an "integral" computer chip to be implanted in his brain. The fact that Bill Clinton and Al Gore have displayed an interest in Wilber's writings tells me all I need to know regarding the relationship between the Globalists' and Wilber's "integral" politics. But again, I still think Wilber is worth reading. If you check my Spiritual Reading List, in the appendix, you'll see that he's on it. And if you Google "Ken Wilber and integral politics," you'll quickly be able to check out the four-quadrant framework and the eight-level spiral dynamics hierarchy that he promotes.

How about Wilber's Four Quadrants?

Wilber's four-quadrant model—*Interior-Individual (Intentional), Exterior-Individual (Behavioral), Interior-Collective (Cultural), Exterior-Collective (Social)*—is a useful tool for understanding the individual-collective dialectic or interplay. But it isn't the ideal framework for understanding sociopolitical reality. The ideal framework for achieving this understanding is Ayn Rand's two pairs of poles: *individualism-statism*, and *capitalism-socialism*. And these two pairs of poles, or four *isms*, provide us with the true "four quadrants" of sociopolitical reality. Let's now consider these poles and see how they apply to democratic and republican political systems.

If you believe in a *democratic* political system, the primacy of the government or a voting majority over the individual, then you are, by definition, a *statist*. By subscribing to this statist model of rule, you have, explicitly or implicitly, embraced a lynch-mob mentality, the fascist mindset that an individual is no more than a de facto slave, a government-owned human animal meant to be sacrificed to the dictates or decrees of the State or a voting majority. If, on the other hand, you believe in a *republican* political system, in inviolable, constitutionally guaranteed individual rights that the State cannot usurp, then you are an *individualist*. As such, your mentality is that of a sovereign man, an individual whose allegiance is to rationality and freedom rather than to a State that in any way seeks to limit or compromise human sovereignty.

But sovereignty must be limited. Otherwise, individuals and gangs could rape, murder, and pillage with no consequences.

If everyone is guaranteed sovereignty, then no one can legally interfere with anyone else's sovereignty or individual rights, including property rights. Sovereignty does not include the right to initiate force against another person or his property. But the State initiates force against citizens by arresting them for victimless crimes (drugs, prostitution, gambling, etc.) and for not paying taxes ("protection money" to the "Mafia-State"). Moreover, it initiates force (theft) against them when it engages in "quantitative easing," which devalues their dollars. Jesus, who was against force and violence, would, in my estimation, be an outspoken critic, or even outright enemy, of today's Mafia-State.

Now let's move on to *capitalism-socialism*. True or laissez-faire capitalism, strictly speaking, is not an economic system; it is a social system based on the trader principle, wherein independent contractors freely exchange goods and services sans the interference of the Mafia-State, the government. Socialism, by contrast, is a social system based on de facto State ownership and control of all goods and services. It is the Mafia model of government fully institutionalized, wherein Big "MoFoBro" owns the fruit of your labor and "gives" you whatever crumbs it wants.

In return for your "service to the State," you receive "protection"—from everything but the tyrannical State itself.

Integral Dialectical Politics

You obviously hate socialism, but isn't there a place for collectivism in a free society?

Voluntary socialism or collectivism is fine. In an individualist-capitalist system, individuals can freely form communes or collectives if they so desire. But in a statist-socialist system, you cannot set up a John Galt-type capitalist community that is independent of the State. Big Brother will insist on regulating your town and taxing your townspeople.

I think the best, or most "integral," way to view this relationship between individualism-capitalism and statism-socialism is as a dialectic, with the former as the thesis and the latter as the antithesis. Because individualism-capitalism *subsumes* statism-socialism (meaning that the former allows for the latter, but not vice-versa), the synthesis that results is an individualist-capitalist system that *sublates* (or subordinates but preserves) the State and allows for *voluntary* collectivism. In other words, in a moral, or "integral," society, the State still exists, but its function is limited to providing national security and protecting and preserving individual rights. In such a society, man *qua* man and man *qua* Son of Man can flourish, creating a terrestrial Shangri-La, "heaven" on earth.

Determining Political Truth

Why should we accept the political picture that you paint? Your ideas seem extreme and radical.

My political ideas or philosophy are no more extreme than the U.S. Constitution. If you think it's a radical document, then you'll probably categorize me as a right-wing nut or ideologue. My invitation to you is to compare and contrast the preeminent "radical" left-wing literature with that of the right wing, and determine political truth for yourself. That's what I've done. My specialized area of study in college was Marxism. And I studied it under the foremost neo-Marxist academic in the world, Herbert Marcuse (1898-1979). By all means read Marcuse's *One-Dimensional Man*, Marx's *The Communist Manifesto*, Noam Chomsky's (libertarian socialist) writings, and whatever other left-wing literature appeals to you. Then compare those texts to the seminal right-wing literature. My suggestion is to start with Ron Paul's *The Revolution: A Manifesto*, Ayn Rand's *Capitalism: The Unknown Ideal*, and various essays by Murray Rothbard and other libertarians available online at lewrockwell.com. And if you want to understand the modus operandi of the largest counterfeiting racket in history, read the definitive text on the Federal Reserve, *The Creature from Jekyll Island*, by G. Edward Griffin, and/or watch his Youtube.com videos (*The Creature from Jekyll Island, by G. Edward Griffin*, and *The Collectivist Conspiracy, by G. Edward Griffin*). If you devote yourself to studying and objectively considering the literature and videos I've suggested, you'll not only raise your political IQ, but you just might come to an enlightened conclusion regarding Jesus' politics.

CHAPTER FIFTEEN

Christianity in the Aquarian Age

The Dawning of the Age of Aquarius

Is it true that the Earth has moved into the Age of Aquarius, and if so, what effect will that have on Christianity?

Due to the slow processional movement of its rotation, the Earth moves backward through the celestial Zodiac about thirty degrees, or one zodiacal sign, approximately every 2,150 years. Many professional astrologers believe that the Earth shifted from the constellation Pisces into that of Aquarius in or before the twentieth century, while many others maintain that the shift won't occur for at least another five hundred years. Because the zodiacal territories of Pisces and Aquarius overlap, it is impossible to determine the exact time of the change.

I personally believe that the "dawning" of the Age of Aquarius, coinciding with the Enlightenment, occurred in the eighteenth century, and that since that time the Earth has moved fully into Aquarius. I base my belief on the cultural, sociopolitical, and technological changes that have transpired over the past three hundred years. These changes have challenged the institution of Christianity, a classical Piscean-Age (meaning faith-based) religion that has had to continually adjust its message in response to the emergent Aquarian-Age energy or "vibration." Aquarius' energy rules science and technology, individual liberty and equality, and industrial capitalism and state communism/socialism: all themes, which, on one level or another, represent a challenge to the Church's authority.

The Enlightenment sought to reform society by liberating men from the controlling influences of church and state. The new culture of individual freedom and intellectual inquiry, epitomized by the Declaration of Independence and the U.S. Constitution, augured the ascendance of scientism and the decline of faith-based religion. The discoveries of the conduction of electricity (an Aquarius-ruled energy), in 1729, and of Uranus, the ruling planet of Aquarius, in 1781, further signified the dawning of the Age of Aquarius. In the nineteenth century, Darwin's theory of evolution shook the Church's foundation. And the rise of industrial capitalism similarly threatened the Church's authority, as the burgeoning culture of materialism and consumerism gradually began to supplant the traditional Christian ideals of simplicity and service.

In the nineteenth century, as industrial capitalism took root in Europe, Karl Marx responded with *The Communist Manifesto*, an ideological reaction to the perceived exploitation and dehuman-ization of the working class. Marx's communist ideology gained widespread support among intellectuals, humanitarians, and champions of the proletariat. And in the twentieth century, as Marxist ideology proliferated throughout the world, resulting in revolutions that led to communist and socialistic governments, the influence of the Christian church correspondingly declined. Marxism is an overtly atheistic ideology, which Marx himself made clear when he proclaimed, "Religion is the opiate of the masses." Consequently, while industrial capitalism indirectly challenged the Church by stressing technology and materialism over faith and devotion, state communism/socialism, which promoted the godless Marxist ideology, directly sought to destroy, or at least disempower, not only the Christian Church, but all forms of institutional religion.

In the twentieth century, the movement to undermine the authority of the Christian Church continued, and in the early twenty-first century it accelerated, as notable atheists, such as the late Christopher Hitchens and the biologist Richard Dawkins, mounted full-on intellectual assaults against Christianity. The Christian Church, in turn, has responded by softening and secularizing its message. Consequently, many of its preachers now sound more like New Age self-improvement gurus than Christian ministers. Instead of warning their congregations about the wages of sin and the eternal, infernal Hell that awaits non-believers in Jesus, these ministers offer practical advice for living a positive, conventionally successful life.

Universal "Brotherhood" in the New Age

Is the Aquarian Age the panacea that will lead to universal brotherhood and a true New Age?

Not necessarily. To my taste buds, the current New Age (of Aquarius) movement is hardly a bowl of fresh, delectable cherries; it's more like pabulum or packaged tapioca. Instead of profound Truth doctrines, it proffers assorted versions of dumbed-down Dharma drivel. When a clueless, fogged-out mystic like Eckhart Tolle (Sun sign in Aquarius, by the way) is your movement's shining star, then you know that Dystopia, rather than Utopia, is the likely outcome of your brotherhood-and-unity babble.

Aquarius, like every other astrological sign, has its dark side, or weaknesses. Though usually friendly, it is impersonal and dissociative. I've had a number of Aquarius girlfriends over the years, and not one of them was good at intimate, interpersonal relations. But a positive aspect of the Aquarian vibration is increased tolerance. Most people nowadays don't care what color someone's skin is or if they're tatted up and pierced. Acceptance of differences is a sign of brotherhood—but the lack of communication I see everywhere isn't. People are absorbed in their personal communication devices and abstracted away from meaningful relationship with other humans. Walk into a Starbucks and you'll typically see a room filled with coffee sippers zeroed in on their laptops and oblivious to the world.

Even warfare nowadays has been infected by impersonal Aquarius energy. Instead of human beings killing other human beings, we now have drones doing the dirty work of death. And unlike during the Vietnam War, when television news every day was filled with ghastly war scenes, the plastic, politically correct empty suits in TV land no longer air the grisly horrors perpetrated by America's imperialist war machine. The handful of giant corporations that control the U.S. mainstream media has decided that graphically exposing America's global-aggression game is bad for business. Hence, they push "happy talk" because that means more brain-dead viewers and thus more advertising revenue.

On a worldwide scale, the New World Order "brotherhood" (the international banking cartel and Global Elite) preaches "unity" while simultaneously ripping off the world's wealth and destroying nations' economies in the process. The ideals of brotherhood and unity are admirable—*when they are freely upheld by sovereign individuals.* But when they are *fascistically imposed by the Globalists* as a means to enrich themselves and control the masses, they become destructive to a free social order in which individual rights, including property rights, are sacrosanct.

The True New (Aquarian) Age

The picture you've painted sounds pretty bleak. How can we overcome the negative forces that you've described and establish a true New (Aquarian) Age?

By both living and promoting an integral vision of life. This is essentially a twofold *conscious* process involving *ontology* and *epistemology*. First, *ontologically* (meaning organismically, beyond thought), we must learn to live in the Spirit, to commune with and channel God's Light-energy. Second, *epistemologically* (meaning cognitively in order to attain valid knowledge), we must learn how to think rationally—objectively and logically. This skill is *not* taught in public (or State-funded) schools, because if it were, Big Brother's ass would be cooked, as free (and freedom)-thinking individuals, en masse, would work together to end the Federal Reserve, the IRS, and all the wars of aggression (including the ones against drugs, prostitution, and gambling). And, of course, this skill is *not* taught by the mainstream Church, because if it were, the Church's mission— to convince you, on blind faith, to accept the truth of exoteric Christian dogma—would utterly fail.

In our discussions, you've recommended a number of books on spiritual ontology, mystical metaphysics. My question is: What books do you recommend on epistemology?

First read *Objectivism: The Philosophy of Ayn Rand*, by Leonard Peikoff, then read *Introduction to Objectivist Epistemology*, by Ayn Rand.

But Ayn Rand was a staunch atheist, diametrically opposed to your spiritual vision of life.

Don't throw the baby out with the bathwater. Rand (Sun sign in Aquarius, by the way) was a genius, and you can only benefit from considering her five-branch philosophical hierarchy— metaphysics, epistemology, ethics, politics, and esthetics. I'm convinced that if Rand had been exposed to the highest mystical teachings and been taught how to meditate, she would have married Objectivism with spiritual Dharma and become the ultimate integral guru.

Rand emphasizes the practice of *logic*—"the art of non-contradictory identification of [*phenomenal*] reality." I too emphasize the practice of logic, but unlike Rand, I also emphasize the practice of *onto-logic*—the *spiritual* art of non-contradictory identification with *transphenomenal* (or Ultimate) Reality. *Logic* is the *epistemic method* of right thinking, the establishment of mental relationships that identify reality, and what I call *onto-logic* is the *ontic method* of right "non-thinking," or right non-mental relationship with Reality (as Spirit). Epistemology pertains to *knowing* (about things), and spiritual ontology to *being* (at-one with the *unknowable* "Thing," or Being, Itself). A true integralist marries the arts of logic and onto-logic, and thereby becomes a sage, or Hermetic alchemist.

What do you mean by non-contradictory identification?

Contradictions do not, and cannot, exist in either reality or Reality. Both phenomenal reality and Ultimate Reality are *always* simply as they are. Right epistemology—the art of logic, or non-contradictory identification—enables one to *mentally* identify truth relative to phenomenal reality; *onto-logic*, non-contradictory ontological identification, enables one to *spiritually* identify with Ultimate Reality. Epistemic truth is the identification of phenomenal reality; integral Truth is the recognition of *both* phenomenal reality and Ultimate Reality.

Integral Truth lived means the practice of both onto-logic and logic. It means that one's Plugged-in Presence practice doesn't stop with communion with the Absolute, but that it also extends to deep psychical communion with life, which enables one to make essential mental connections and thereby profoundly grasp relative, or phenomenal, reality. Consciousness *is* relationship. Your "ontological IQ" (as I define it) is your capacity to consciously relate to the Spirit, and your "epistemological IQ" (as I define it) is your capacity to make conscious connections that enable you to identify and grasp reality.

How would "Integral Truth lived" translate into a true New Age?

When a critical mass of people begins to live in the Spirit and to think logically and objectively, then a true New Age Enlightenment would emerge. Ayn Rand's five-branch philosophical hierarchy provides us with a basic framework for understanding how Integral Truth would effect comprehensive sociocultural change. Creatively employing her hierarchy, we have: right *metaphysics* (ontology) = life in the meta-physical Spirit; right *epistemology* = logical, objective thinking; right *ethics* (or morality) = non-aggression; right *politics* = laissez-faire capitalism; right *esthetics* = art that uplifts the spirit. In sum, *right metaphysics* and *right epistemology* naturally translate into *right ethics*, *right politics*, *right esthetics*, and thus *right*, or *integral*, society.

Christianity in the True New Age

How does Christianity fit into this New (Aquarian) Age Enlightenment?

Christianity, like Pisces, is symbolized by the sign of the fish. But the Age of the poor "fish," the brainwashed true believer caught in the net of the conventional Christian Church, is coming to an end. The three dominant new Aquarian-Age "Churches"—the "Church of Science," the "Church of Secular Humanism," and the "Church of the New Age Movement"—have already driven a number of nails into its coffin, which eventually will be buried for good. Prescient ministers, such as superstar pulpiteer Joel

Osteen, who see the future, or lack thereof, of the Church of Fire and Brimstone, have already adapted to the changing zeitgeist; hence, their sermons mimic New Age pep talks and avoid Christian preachments.

But the future *true* New (Aquarian) Age Christian minister will *not* resort to a continuum of pop New Age-type homilies, à la Joel Osteen, to maintain his relevance. Instead, he will teach Electrical Christianity, the practice of Plugged-in Presence, *true* Holy Communion. The new Electrical Christian Church will not be about faith-based *sheeple* mindlessly accepting the Bible as the Word of God; it will be about free-thinking *individuals* intelligently communing with the Spirit and radiating its electrical-like Energy.

The glyph for the sign of Aquarius is two parallel wavy lines. The *wavy* lines symbolize unconventional energy, energy making waves in society. The fact that the lines are parallel signifies that this unconventional energy seeks to create consonance or harmony rather than dissonance or disharmony. Aquarius energy is electrical in nature; thus, one could say it is "written in the stars" that in the Age of Aquarius, Christianity will morph from a Piscean religion, symbolized by two fish swimming in opposite directions, into an Aquarian one based on the principles of electricity, symbolized by waves of energy.

What about challenges from the three dominant new Aquarian-Age "Churches" you just mentioned?

The "Churches" of Science, Secular Humanism, and the pop New Age Movement represent no threat to Electrical Christianity because its Dharma is unassailable, beyond the reach of deconstruction. Because Electrical Christianity is not a belief system, but simply a radical empirical method to unfold, or de-contract, consciousness (the divine "element" of the human soul), ultimately, there is nothing to deconstruct but consciousness itself. And because consciousness itself is always and only the unknowable subject and never a cognizable object, it is forever immune to deconstruction.

What about the Holy Spirit? Science does not acknowledge its existence.

The *New Oxford American Dictionary* defines *spirit* as "the soul." Ayn Rand defines *spirit* as "pertaining to consciousness." In other words, *spirit* is just another word for *soul* or *consciousness*, and as such, spirit itself is likewise beyond the purview of science. In reality, the proper definition of spirit is the "*energy* of consciousness." And when one's consciousness, or soul, is utterly de-contracted (and thus Whole), then, spontaneously, Whole Energy—the Holy Spirit—moves into and through one's bodymind. Just as an electric current cannot be divorced from the voltage that produces it, likewise the Holy Spirit cannot be separated from the Whole (or uncontracted) consciousness that evokes it. In short, the soul-spirit dyad is an axiomatic irreducible primary, which can be lived and realized, but never reified and analyzed; hence, science can neither acknowledge nor deny its existence.

So Electrical Christianity represents humanity's salvation in the Aquarian Age?

Absolutely. Even skeptical scientists and avowed atheists can practice Electrical Christianity. This is the case because Electrical Christianity is not a religion per se, but rather a universal method or Way to achieve liberation on every level of human existence. The Electrical Christian technique of Plugged-in Presence, or Holy Communion, establishes one in right (or direct and immediate) relationship, which connects one not only to the Spirit, but also to other humans, thereby fostering the ethos of *organic individualist*, rather than *artificial statist*, brotherhood and unity. But if most humans (such as those encamped in a Starbucks) are perpetually absorbed in cyberspace or their electronic gizmos rather than engaged in communion with the Whole, then universal human interconnectedness cannot occur, and man's "social salvation" will remain just a dream.

The discipline of Electrical Christianity *spiritually* liberates individuals, enabling them to awaken as Christs (meaning "anointed," or Blessed, souls). If everyone were taught the Electrical Christian practice of Plugged-in Presence, then the Grace shed on the world would be immensely magnified, and Christs, or Buddhas, would abound. Religious differences would dissolve, because a Spirit-full disciple has no attachment to a particular religion, and thus no need to defend a doctrinal belief system.

And if this practice of Plugged-in Presence were extended from the domain of ontology, or Spirit, to that of epistemology, or mind, then mankind's liberation would be total, as free-thinking individuals, en masse, would remake the social order in accord with ideals expounded by the likes of political savants Ron Paul, Ayn Rand, and Murray Rothbard. There would be separation of Church and State and separation of Economy and State, but there would be no separation among the hearts of the sovereign people.

The Electrical Dharma Revolution

What can we do to awaken humanity to the Electrical Spiritual Dharma?

First, live the Dharma. Strive to become a Christ or Buddha, a living example of an en-Light-ened being. Second, study the Dharma. Read the Great Spiritual Traditions, and learn to express the One Truth from multiple angles. This will enable you to intelligently engage both avowed atheists and Bible-thumping Christians, and everyone in between these two "extremes." Third, teach your potential converts the Plugged-in Presence method of meditation. Generally speaking, when you engage mainstream Christians, you'll want to teach it to them in the form of the Eucharist, or Holy Communion; and when you engage atheists or science-minded individuals, you'll want to present it as Ohm's Law applied to consciousness and its energy. Fourth, give them a copy of *Electrical Christianity* to read.

Eckhart Tolle, the pop New Age guru, envisions a "New Earth," and Ken Wilber, the New Age pandit, promotes an "Integral World," but what I'm offering is a revolution—an Electrical Dharma Revolution that will enable everyone to plug into the Source and pull down the true power of Now, Light-energy from above. This Light-energy, in conjunction with enlightened (or rational) thinking, will en-Light-en the planet. My invitation to you is to join this revolution and help awaken humanity from the darkness of today to the Light of tomorrow, the *true* New (Aquarian) Age.

Spiritual Reading List

Advaita Vedanta

<u>Highly Recommended</u>

Ashtavakra Gita, trans. Hari Prasad Shastri. (Timeless Advaita Vedanta text. Available at www.shantisadan.org. Other translations also available.)

Be As You Are: The Teachings of Ramana Maharshi, David Godman. (Best introductory book on the teachings of Ramana Maharshi.)

Sat-Darshana Bhashya and Talks with Maharshi, Sri Ramanasramam. (A learned devotee's in-depth consideration of Ramana Maharshi's teachings within the framework of Indian-yogic philosophy.)

Sri Ramana Gita, Ramana Maharshi. (An utterly unique, ultra-profound text that details the function of the Amrita Nadi in the Self-realization process.)

Talks with Sri Ramana Maharshi, Ramana Maharshi. ("Must" reading. A truly great and inspiring book. Avoid the dumbed-down version published by Inner Directions.)

(*Sat-Darshana Bhashya*, *Sri Ramana Gita*, and *Talks With Sri Ramana Maharshi* are available at www.arunachala.org.)

<u>Recommended</u>

I Am That: Talks with Sri Nisargadatta Maharaj, Maurice Frydman. (Classic, über-popular text.)

Vivekachudamani (Crest Jewel of Discrimination), trans. Swami Prabhavananda and Christopher Isherwood. (Other translations of Shankara's teachings also available.)

Buddhism (Original)

<u>Highly Recommended</u>

Some Sayings of the Buddha, F.L. Woodward. (Easily the finest presentation of the Buddha's core teachings.)

<u>Recommended</u>

Buddhism: An Outline of its Teachings and Schools, Hans Wolfgang Schuman. (Solid academic book.)

In the Buddha's Words: An Anthology of Discourses from the Pali Canon, Bhikku Bodhi. (Excellent, comprehensive introduction to the Buddha's teachings.)

Mindfulness in Plain English, Venerable Henepola Gunaratana. (Best introductory text on insight meditation.)

The Heart of Buddhist Meditation, Nyaponika Thera. (Classic text on insight meditation.)

The Living Thoughts of Gotama the Buddha, Ananda Coomaraswamy and I.B. Horner. (Classic text. Excellent introduction to Buddhism.)

The Way of Non-Attachment, Dhiravamsa. (Unique Krishnamurti-influenced book on Insight meditation. Out of print.)

Buddhism (Tibetan)

<u>Highly Recommended</u>

Teachings of Tibetan Yoga, Gharma C.C. Chang. (Superb Mahamudra presentation. "Must" reading for serious meditators.)

The Cycle of Day and Night, Namkhai Norbu. (Outstanding Dzogchen meditation manual. "Must" reading for serious meditators.)

The Golden Letters, John Myrdhin Reynolds. (Scholarly exposition of the history and practice of Dzogchen in relation to the Garab Dorje, the first teacher of Dzogchen.)

The Precious Treasury of the Way of Abiding, Longchen Rabjam. (Marvelous ultra-mystical text by a revered Vajrayana master. If you appreciate this book, get *A Treasure Trove of Scriptural Transmission: A Commentary on The Precious Treasury of the Basic Space of Phenomena*, by the same author. Other translations/annotations of Rabjam's texts are available.)

The Supreme Source, Namkhai Norbu. (The fundamental tantric text of Dzogchen.)

Recommended

Cutting Through Spiritual Materialism, Chogyam Trungpa. (Enlightening text by a modern "crazy wisdom" master.)

Naked Awareness, Karma Chagme. (Excellent material on Dzogchen and Mahamudra.)

Self-Liberation Though Seeing With Naked Awareness, John Myrdhin Reynolds. (Compare this translation of/commentary on Padmasambhava's *Yoga of Knowing the Mind and Seeing Reality* to W.Y. Evans-Wentz's in *The Tibetan Book of the Great Liberation*.)

The Tibetan Book of the Great Liberation, W.Y. Evans-Wentz. (Classic translation of/commentary on Padmasambhava's *Yoga of Knowing the Mind and Seeing Reality*. Compare this translation/commentary to John Myrdhin Reynolds's in *Self-Liberation Through Seeing With Naked Awareness*. Skip Carl Jung's ridiculous "Psychological Commentary.")

Tibetan Yoga and Secret Doctrines, W.Y. Evans-Wentz. (Classic, ultra-mystical text.)

Wonders of the Natural Mind, Tenzin Wangyal. (The essence of Dzogchen in the Native Bon Tradition of Tibet.)

Buddhism (Zen)

Highly Recommended

The Diamond Sutra and the Sutra of Hui Neng, trans. A.F. Price. (Other translations of these timeless sutras also available.)

The Zen Teaching of Huang Po, John Blofeld. (Easily the best book on Zen.)

Recommended

Kensho, The Heart of Zen, Thomas Cleary. (My favorite Cleary text on Zen.)

The Practice of Zen, Gharma C.C. Chang. (Great autobiographical accounts of enlightenment. Out of print.)

The Way of Zen, Alan Watts. (Classic introductory text by the godfather of American Zen.)

The Three Pillars of Zen, Philip Kapleau. (Classic, popular Rinzai Zen text that emphasizes the *satori* experience.)

Tracing Back the Radiance: Chinul's Korean Way of Zen, Robert Buswell, Jr. (Outstanding account of a great Zen master's spiritual evolution.)

Zen Mind, Beginner's Mind, Shunryu Suzuki. (Classic, ultra-popular Soto Zen text.)

Zen Teaching of Instantaneous Awakening, Ch'an Master Hui Hai; trans. John Blofeld. (Fine Dharma instructions by a great Chinese Ch'an master.)

(Scholarly types will enjoy Heinrich Dumoulin's *Zen Buddhism: A History (India and China)* and *Zen Buddhism: A History (Japan)*, Vol. 2. Serious students of Buddhist philosophy will appreciate Gharma C.C.

Chang's *The Buddhist Teaching of Totality*, which expounds Hwa Yen Buddhism's wonderful, all-embracing philosophy in relation to Zen. If you enjoy reading Zen, check out Thomas Cleary's numerous books at Amazon.com.)

Christianity, Judaism, and Gnosticism

<u>Highly Recommended</u>

Meditations on the Tarot, Valentin Tomberg. (An astonishing journey into Christian Hermeticism. "Must" reading for anyone interested in Christian mysticism.)

Meister Eckhart. (*The Complete Mystical Works of Meister Eckhart* is the book I recommend—but it costs $98. *Meister Eckhart*, trans. Raymond B. Blakney, is a fine compilation of Eckhart's sermons, and goes for about $15. Scholarly types will want to supplement either of the aforementioned books with *The Mystical Thought of Meister Eckhart*, by Bernard McGinn.)

Mysticism, Evelyn Underwood. (Wonderful, classic, early twentieth-century text by the first lady of Christian mysticism.)

The Foundations of Mysticism. Bernard McGinn. (Extraordinary presentation of the Western mystical tradition. "Must" reading for scholarly types.)

<u>Recommended</u>

Inner Christianity, Richard Smoley. (Clear and thoughtful guide to the esoteric Christian tradition.)

Jewish Meditation, Aryeh Kaplan.

Open Mind, Open Heart, Thomas Keating. (Classic, best-selling text on the Gospel's contemplative dimension.)

The Big Book of Christian Mysticism: The Essential Guide to Contemplative Spirituality, Carl McColman. (Good introductory text and resource guide for those interested in Christian mysticism.)

The Mystic Christ, Ethan Walker. (Excellent book for Christians.)

The Practice of the Presence of God, Brother Lawrence, Robert Edmondson, and Jonathon Wilson-Hartgrove. (Classic text on the practice of establishing a conscious relationship with the Divine.)

The Secret Book of John, trans. Stevan Davies.

The Sermon on the Mount According to Vedanta, Swami Prabhavananda.

The Way of a Pilgrim and the Pilgrim Continues His Way, Multiple fine translations available. (Inspiring book for practitioners of prayer and mantra meditation.)

(Scholarly types into Western Christian mysticism will love all the fine texts by Prof. Bernard McGinn. Check out McGinn's *The Presence of God: A History of Western Mysticism* series. This four-volume series includes *The Foundations of Mysticism* (highly recommended), *The Growth of Mysticism*, *The Flowering of Mysticism*, and *The Crisis of Mysticism*. Beyond this series, McGinn has also graced us with *The Essential Writings of Christian Mysticism*, an immensely rich anthology of the greatest Christian mystical literature. Selections in this volume include writings from such great mystics as Origen, Augustine, Pseudo-Dionysius the Areopagite, St. John of the Cross, Bernard of Clairvaux, Meister Eckhart, John Ruusbroec, and many more. Relative to a scholarly consideration of Jewish mysticism, I also recommend Gershom Scholem's *Major Trends in Jewish Mysticism*. Not only is this text the canonical modern work on the nature and history of Jewish mysticism, but it is also a thoughtful and incisive academic consideration of mysticism in general.)

Daism

Highly Recommended

Hridaya Rosary (Four Thorns of Heart-Instruction), Adi Da Samraj. (Excellent technical devotional-meditation book.)

The Knee of Listening, Adi Da Samraj. (Best spiritual autobiography ever written. "Must" reading for mystics. Get a copy of the latest edition, but also get a copy of an earlier edition written under either the names of Franklin Jones or Bubba Free John. These earlier editions, unlike later and current editions, contain Da's outstanding "Meditation of Understanding," instructions on the practice of "real meditation," or "radical understanding.")

The Liberator: The "Radical" Reality-Teachings of The Great Avataric Sage, Adi Da Samraj, Adi Da Samraj.

The Method of the Siddhas, Adi Da Samraj. (A truly great spiritual book. Out of print and only available used. Try to get a copy written under the names of either Franklin Jones or Bubba Free John. The current revised edition of the book, entitled *My "Bright" Word*, lacks the direct visceral impact of the original text.)

The Pneumaton, Adi Da Samraj. (Ultra-esoteric consideration of "Pneuma," the Spirit.)

The Way of Perfect Knowledge: The "Radical" Practice of Transcendental Spirituality in the Way of Adidam, Adi Da Samraj.

Recommended

He-And-She Is Me: The Indivisibility of Consciousness and Light In the Divine Body of the Ruchira Avatar, Adi Da Samraj.

Ruchira Avatara Hridaya-Siddha Yoga: The Divine (and Not Merely Cosmic) Spiritual Baptism in the Way of Adidam, Adi Da Samraj.

Santosha Adidam: The Essential Summary of the Divine Way of Adidam, Adi Da Samraj.

The All-Completing and Final Divine Revelation To Mankind: A Summary Description Of The Supreme Yoga Of The Seventh Stage Of Life In The Divine Way Of Adidam, Adi Da Samraj.

(The four books on the Recommended List contain a number of the same essays. Nonetheless, each book includes enough unique material to merit its reading.)

Hinduism (Yoga)

<u>Highly Recommended</u>

The Bhagavad Gita, translations by Eknath Easwaran, Swami Prabahvananda and Christopher Isherwood, S. Radakrishnan. (Many other fine translations/annotations also available.)

The Yoga of Spiritual Devotion: A Modern Translation of the Narada Bhakti Sutras, Prem Prakesh. (A simple, inspiring text on the spiritual path of love and devotion.)

Yoga Philosophy of Patanjali, Swami Hariharananda Aranya. (The best account of classical yoga I've encountered. Many other fine translations/annotations also available.)

<u>Recommended</u>

Be Here Now, Baba Ram Dass. (Classic introductory book on Eastern philosophy. An easy and entertaining read.)

How to Know God, Prabhavananda and Isherwood. (Best introduction to the yoga philosophy of Patanjali.)

The Essential Swami Ramdas, Swami Ramdas. (Inspiring writings of a great twentieth-century *bhakti* yogi.)

The Gospel of Sri Ramakrishna, Swami Nikhilananda. (A revered *bhakti* classic.)

The Synthesis of Yoga, Sri Aurobindo. (Profound essays on yoga by Sri Aurobindo, the renowned twentieth-century Indian guru-philosopher. If you appreciate this book and crave more Aurobindo, get a copy of *The Life Divine*.)

The Upanishads, translations by Mascara, and by Prabhavananda and Isherwood. (Other fine translations also available.)

The Yoga Tradition, Georg Feuerstein. (Outstanding reference book on the history, literature, philosophy, and practice of yoga.)

Kashmir Shaivism

<u>Highly Recommended</u>

Pratyabhijnahrdayam: The Secret of Self-Recognition, Jaideva Singh. (The basic introductory handbook to the abstruse philosophical system of recognition. Not for the intellectually challenged.)

Siva Sutras: The Yoga of Supreme Identity, Jaideva Singh. (The foundational text of Kashmir Shaivism.)

The Doctrine of Vibration, Mark S.G. Dyczkowski. (A scholarly analysis of the doctrines and practices of Kashmir Shaivism.)

The Philosophy of Sadhana, Deba Brata SenSharma. (Outstanding text that deals clearly and extensively with the ultra-important topic of *Shaktipat*, the Descent of Divine Power, or Grace. "Must" reading for serious mystics.)

The Triadic Heart of Siva, Paul Eduardo Muller-Ortega. (An ultra-esoteric text about the Heart (Hridaya) as Ultimate Reality, Emissional Power, and Embodied Cosmos.)

<u>Recommended</u>

Kundalini, The Energy of the Depths, Lilian Silburn. (As an Amazon.com reviewer puts it, "The foremost modern exposition of Kundalini.")

Spanda Karikas: The Divine Creative Pulsation, Jaideva Singh. (An elaboration of the dynamic aspect of Transcendental Consciousness.)

Miscellaneous

<u>Highly Recommended</u>

The First and Last Freedom, J. Krishnamurti. ("Must" reading for all mystics. If you appreciate this book and want to read more Krishnamurti, get his multivolume *Commentaries on Living*.)

Introduction to Objectivist Epistemology, Ayn Rand. ("Must" reading for all mystics.)

Objectivism: The Philosophy of Ayn Rand, Leonard Peikoff. ("Must" reading for all mystics.)

The Way of Chuang Tzu, Thomas Merton. (Other translations also available.)

<u>Recommended</u>

A Brief History of Everything, Ken Wilber. (If you're interested in "integral thinking," you'll enjoy this book. If you appreciate it, get *Sex, Ecology, Spirituality: The Spirit of Evolution*.)

Alan Oken's Complete Astrology, Alan Oken. (Best overall book on astrology.)

Ayurveda: The Science of Self-Healing, Vasant Lad. (Fascinating and enlightening exposition of the principles and practical applications of Indian Ayurveda, the oldest healing system in the world.)

Awaken Healing Energy Through the Tao, Mantak Chia. (Classic introductory handbook to the practice and principles of Taoist energy-yoga.)

Return to the One: Plotinus's Guide to God-Realization, Brian Hines. (Accessible modern exposition of an ancient classic, the *Enneads*. Also check out the Armstrong and Mackenna translations at Amazon.com.)

The Mystique of Enlightenment: The Radical Ideas of U.G. Krishnamurti, U.G. Krishnmurti (U.G. was the ultimate spiritual iconoclast. Jean Klein called him "pathological." I call him "a great read.")

The Perennial Philosophy, Aldous Huxley. (Classic text by a great writer.)

The Tao Te Ching. (Numerous translations available.

CPSIA information can be obtained at www.ICGtesting.com
Printed in the USA
BVOW07s2006270614

357605BV00001B/79/P